Endorsements

"After hearing Bob Weiner's endorsement of Martin Powell's book MoneyMatters in My Kingdom, I was expecting it to be awesome, but I was still surprised by how good it actually was. This is the best book I've ever read on secular or Christian finance."

Rick Joyner, MorningStar Ministries

"Many books have been written on prosperity, but few authors have linked the idea of prosperity to a God given plan that will advance God's Kingdom. Like a skillful surgeon, Pastor Martin cuts through all the inaccurate mindsets concerning prosperity and equips the reader to become a fine-tuned custodian of God's power to create wealth. Pastor Martin has written a masterpiece to prepare the character of God's people for the greatest transfer of wealth which will influence society with the Gospel of the Kingdom. The principles and patterns in this book will encourage you to take the necessary steps to reconfigure your mindsets in alignment with God's purpose for your life. *Money Matters: In My Kingdom* is an anointed map that will guide you into the ways of provision to fulfill God's vision for your life. Enjoy!"

Mark Kauffman, Jubilee Ministries International, Global Mega Impact Corporation, New Castle, Pennsylvania

"Martin Powell explains very clearly what the world is facing today regarding global economics and the risks we all face. Martin provides a simple concept of how to prepare for the future and to be the stewards that God has called each of us to be with our resources."

Lt. General (R) William G. Boykin,
U.S. Army

"What a joy to recommend Martin Powell's new book *Money Matters: In My Kingdom*. Martin clearly understands God's original great commission listed in Genesis 12:3 that though Abraham and his seed every nation would be blessed. We are Abraham's seed given the power to make wealth so that every nation would be blessed and every person could hear the good news of Jesus. Thank you Martin for your wonderful book filled with practical revelation which clearly lays out a plan of action for these exciting days ahead. Everything we need has already been given in the spiritual world by our wonderful Heavenly Father before the foundation of the world, by His wonderful grace and all we have to do is walk by faith and not by sight and everything He has already provided will be released now into our lives!"

Bob Weiner, Weiner International

"This book is a ground breaking revelation based on the sound principle of God's word and practical experience gained through many years of working with God. I recommend to every believer desiring to stand on sound principles and to enjoy the benefits of God's prosperity to get a copy of this book. Pastor Martin Powell has given us a greater insight while also helping us to come back to basics and prosperity God's way."

Bishop Simon Iheanacho, Presiding Bishop,
UK World Evangelism Churches

"Biblical prosperity is the covenant birthright of every disciple of Christ. Martin Powell has threaded the needle to deliver balanced teaching keys and understanding to point us to not only prosperity but stewardship."

Dr. Bruce Cook, Convener, KEYS,
Austin, Texas

"Bravo! Pastor Powell has written an eloquent, well-balanced, and Scripturally-based treatise on a topic which oftentimes lends itself to extremism within the church. But to characterize this book as one that teaches solely on prosperity would be doing it a great disservice as it covers many fundamental tenets of Christianity itself. I highly recommend it to all believers."

Peter Han, Co-Founder Investingwithinsight.com,
entrepreneur, consultant, and investor

"Martin Powell addresses key issues with a genuine concern for biblical truth. In a world where financial opinions abound, it is good to have a strong foundation in God's word."

Dr. Hugh Osgood, President,
Churches in Communities International

Pastor Martin Powell

Money
Matters:
in My Kingdom

Money Matters: In My Kingdom

Published by:

Kingdom Talents Publishing

375 Star Light Drive

Fort Mill, SC 29715

www.kingdom-talents.com

ISBN 978-1481267052

Copyright © 2011 by Martin Powell

Printed in the United States of America
Second printing. 2012

To correspond with Pastor Martin Powell, please send your letter via email to: GloryandBlessing@gmail.com. You may also contact us in writing at: Pastor Martin Powell, c/o Christ's Mandate for Missions, P.O. Box 7705, Charlotte, NC 28241.

We would love to hear from you, and welcome your comments and thoughts about this book. If you desire Martin to come and minister the Word of God and perform his music in your Church, please mention this when you write.

This book is dedicated to:

Jesus

and

Janet Powell

Special thanks to:

Louise Allen
Gwen Cattron
DeniseAnn Crenshaw
Norma Aguilar
Sherry Yarbrough

Contents

Preface

We are in unprecedented financial turmoil as the earth goes through the birth pains of the revealing of the sons of God and the ushering in of the new age, the Millennium, when Jesus will reign from Jerusalem.

Let us not fall by ignorance of His Word, but be mighty in deeds for Him who is indeed worthy.

Some of us will die for our testimonies, myself included, and others will rise up determined to preach the truth of the gospel of Christ.

Stand in the truth, and after you have done all to stand, stand.

Pastor Martin Powell

Introduction

Money Matters: In My Kingdom has been compiled from years of preaching notes and Bible studies that I have written. As a result, occasionally the reader will find some repetition of material. I felt it would conflict with the integrity of the individual chapters if I were to remove the repetitious material from the text. Therefore, I have retained it in the hope that the repetition will serve to emphasize the key points in the teaching.

This book is not a get-rich-quick book. Rather, it aims to set out the principles through which God prospers His people. Please remember, if you want to get rich quick, you may find that you will ultimately shipwreck your faith!

We find many warnings about trying to get rich quickly throughout the Bible. Let's take a look at some of them:

> "A faithful man will abound with blessings, but whoever *hastens to be rich* will not go unpunished" (Prov. 28:20 New King James Version).

> "So are the ways of every one that is *greedy of gain*; which taketh away the life of the owners thereof" (Prov. 1:19).

> "Let your character be free from *the love* of money, being content with what you have; for He Himself has said, 'I will never desert you, nor will I ever forsake you'" (Heb. 13:5 New American Standard Bible).

"... men of corrupt minds and destitute of the truth, *who suppose that godliness is a means of gain.* From such withdraw yourself. Now godliness with contentment is great gain. For we brought nothing into this world, and it is certain we can carry nothing out. And having food and clothing, with these we shall be content. But *those who desire to be rich* fall into temptation and a snare, and into many foolish and harmful lusts which drown men in destruction and perdition. For *the love of money is a root of all kinds of evil*" (Tim. 6:5-10 NKJV).

"No one can serve two masters; for either he will hate the one and love the other, or else he will be loyal to the one and despise the other. *You cannot serve God and mammon.* Therefore I say to you, do not worry about your life, what you will eat or what you will drink... For after all these things the Gentiles seek. For your heavenly Father knows that you need all these things. *But seek first the kingdom of God and His righteousness*, and all these things shall be added to you" (Matt. 6:24-33).

We have many warnings from the Bible about the love of money and trying to get rich quickly. Certainly there is nothing wrong with being rich, but our hearts need to be pure. We must follow God's priorities, and He commands us to *"Seek first the Kingdom of God."* We cannot serve both mammon and God. (See Matt. 6:24.) We must make the right choices. When we choose to put God's kingdom first, we will be able to prosper.

In order to further the Kingdom of God, His children must prosper. In this way money will be made available for multitudes of ministries, whether it is a television or radio ministry, an overseas evangelism crusade, a hospital, a Christian school, a Bible college, or any other type of outreach. Money will be available to advance the Kingdom of God when His children prosper financially by seeking first His Kingdom in their lives.

The majority of us spend many hours a week in an effort to earn money, so let us be wise by taking heed to the true wisdom of how to prosper, through believing the Scriptures that God has set forth in His Word.

Pastor Martin Powell

Chapter 1

God's Heart on Prosperity

Jesus Was Slain to Receive Riches!

> "Saying with a loud voice, Worthy is the Lamb that was slain to receive power, *and riches*, and wisdom, and strength, and honour, and glory, and blessing." (Rev. 5:12)

If our Lord and Savior went to the cross in order to receive power, riches, and blessing, should we not endeavor to understand and receive these things that He has bought for us at such a cost?

Sometimes it seems to me that the fear of riches and greed, accompanied with short- sighted self-righteousness, prevent us from having the blessings Jesus so painfully bought for us.

> "Woe to you lawyers! For you have taken away the key of knowledge. You did not enter in yourselves, and those who were entering in you hindered." (Luke 11:52 NKJV)

What is God's heart with regard to prosperity? Does He want us to prosper, or does He want us to live a life of poverty?

"Let them shout for joy, and be glad, that favour my
righteous cause: yea, let them say continually, Let the
LORD be magnified, *which hath pleasure* in the prosperity of his servant." (Ps. 35:27)

It says quite clearly here that the Lord has pleasure in the prosperity of His servant. In fact He has asked us to say this continually! Why would we bother to say something continually? We
would do so because sometimes we must say a truth many times
before we will actually believe it.

God's Thoughts about Prosperity

Let's take a look at the New Testament. Have God's thoughts
regarding prosperity changed?

The Greek word that is translated as "prosper" in the English
New Testament is εὐοδόω, pronounced *euodoo*. There are at
least two meanings for this word: "to help on the road" and "to
succeed in business affairs."

This Greek word is used in only three verses in the New Testament:

"For God is my witness, whom I serve with my spirit
in the gospel of his Son, that without ceasing I make
mention of you always in my prayers; Making request, if by any means now at length I might have *a
prosperous* journey by the will of God to come unto
you" (Rom. 1:9).

"Upon the first day of the week let every one of you
lay by him in store, as God hath *prospered* him, that
there be no gatherings when I come" (1 Cor.16:1-2).

"Beloved, I wish above all things that thou mayest *prosper* and be in health, even as thy soul *prospereth*" (3 John 1:2).

This last verse was written by God through John to the well-beloved Gaius. We can certainly believe that the contents of this verse are speaking to us, as well.

"All scripture is given by inspiration of God, and is profitable for doctrine, for reproof, for correction, for instruction in righteousness" (2 Tim. 3:16).

Therefore, we see that John was inspired of God to write this Scripture (3 John 1:2). Realizing this, we can digest its contents to see what our Father is saying to us.

"I wish above all things that thou mayest prosper." This is a very strong statement. Does God want us to prosper above all things? The simple answer to this question is, "No." The Scripture goes on to say, ". . . *even* as thy soul prospereth." This word *even* is the word καθώς, pronounced *kathos* in the Greek, and it means "according to, inasmuch, in proportion to."

Here we see that God is like any other father. He wants His children to prosper physically in proportion to the prosperity of their souls. God does not give prosperity to spiritual babies, but He does so as they mature spiritually. You would not give a car to a three-year-old, and you would not give a child everything it said it wanted. God has set it in order that our souls must prosper first, and then we prosper physically in proportion to the prosperity that is experienced by our souls. The Father does not want spoiled children.

"Now I say, That the heir, as long as he is a child, differeth nothing from a servant, though he be lord of all; But is under tutors and governors until the time appointed of the father." (Gal. 4:1)

Was Jesus Rich or Poor?

When Jesus came into the world, how did His Father provide for Him?

> "And when they were come into the house, they saw the young child with Mary his mother, and fell down, and worshipped him: and when they had opened their treasures, they presented unto him gifts; gold, and frankincense, and myrrh." (Matt. 2:11)

As we read the above Scripture, we learn that Jesus was well provided for. The Wise Men gave Him gifts from their treasures. In January 2011, gold was worth $1,416 per ounce, the weight of a typical gold coin. How many gold coins (though the gold may not have been in the form of coins) do you think they brought for Jesus? Did they simply "flip one to Him" between them all? No, they were very generous in their gifts to the King of kings.

It is easy to see, therefore, that the Father provided well for Joseph and Mary in looking after Jesus.

So why do people say that Jesus was poor?

> "For ye know the grace of our Lord Jesus Christ, that, though he was rich, yet for your sakes he became poor, that ye through his poverty might be rich." (2 Cor. 8:9)

Here it says quite clearly that the Lord Jesus Christ was rich. This word "rich" in the Greek is πλούσιος, *plousios*, which means: "wealthy, abounding with."

In *Strong's Exhaustive Concordance* we find reference 4145, which reads as follows: "plousios; wealthy; fig. abounding with—rich."

Yes, it was for our sake that Jesus became poor. Why did He do this? He became poor, that we could become rich!

Becoming poor was *a choice* that Jesus made for us. He sacrificed His wealth so that we might become wealthy. What a transaction! He surrendered His riches and became poor so that we could get out of our poverty and become rich.

So when did He become poor? We said earlier that He had many people providing for His needs.

> "And many women were there beholding afar off, which followed Jesus from Galilee, ministering unto him: Among which was Mary Magdalene, and Mary the mother of James and Joses, and the mother of Zebedee's children." (Matt. 27:54-56)

Jesus led a ministry team that had a treasurer, and they had enough money to always give to the poor. This abundance that the Father gave to Jesus even took into account that the treasurer of the team was a thief!

> "But Judas Iscariot, said, 'Why was this ointment not sold for three hundred denarii and given to the poor?' He said this, not because he cared about the poor, but because he was a thief, and having charge of the mon-

eybag he used to help himself to what was put into it."
(John 12:4-6 English Standard Version)

Let's ask the question again: When did Jesus become poor?

It happened when He went to the cross, where He was stripped
of everything. But let us remember, Jesus could have avoided
the cross if He had wanted to.

> "Thinkest thou that I cannot now pray to my Father,
> and he shall presently give me more than twelve le-
> gions of angels?" (Matt. 26:53)

Jesus died so that we could have life. But do you think in going to death He stayed there? No, He was raised from the dead.
Likewise, in becoming poor at the cross, Jesus received His
wealth back, and He received even more when He was raised
from the dead.

> "Saying with a loud voice, Worthy is the Lamb that
> was slain to receive power, *and riches*, and wisdom,
> and strength, and honour, and glory, and blessing."
> (Rev. 5:12)

Jesus was Slain to Receive Riches!!

> "And Jesus came and spake unto them, saying, All
> power is given unto me in heaven and in earth."
> (Matt. 28:18)

When we say that Jesus was poor as an example of suffering to
us, we are denying the purpose of His death. Often, many seem
to forget that Jesus is alive now. His death, which took place approximately 2,000 years ago, was only momentary. He truly is

alive now, and all power has been given to Him *on earth*. He has received the riches that He died for.

Let us also remember that like Joseph, Job, and Jesus, we may be called upon to temporarily suffer for the Kingdom's sake, but the end result for us will be the same as it was for them. A plant that has been pruned will always bear more fruit!

Why, then, does teaching on prosperity get knocked around so much in some Christian quarters? I believe the answer can be found in the Book of Zechariah:

> "Thus saith the LORD of hosts; *My cities through prosperity shall yet be spread abroad*;" (Zech. 1:17).

Our enemy does not want Christians to have power and wealth. We must be careful to understand that prosperity does not mean greed! Prosperity and greed are two different words. Prosperity provides the means to spread the Gospel of Jesus Christ across the world. "*My cities through prosperity shall yet be spread abroad.*"

Every Bible, every mission field, every airplane ticket, and every hall that is booked requires money! Every preacher and every preacher's family needs money! Every church and hospital that must be built requires funding! Every radio and TV broadcast costs money!

We cannot buy souls, but we can give our money to help them hear the Word.

Let us, for goodness' sake, get our heads out of the sand and see that God has provided a way for us to spread the Gospel of Jesus Christ to every city in the world.

"But thou shalt remember the LORD thy God: for it is he that giveth thee power to get wealth, that he may establish his covenant which he sware unto thy fathers, as it is this day." (Deut. 8:18)

What Does the Word "Prosperity" Mean?

In the King James Version of the Bible, there are nine words in Hebrew, one word in Aramaic, and one word in Greek that are used for "prosperity."

The Greek word for "prosperity" defines the word in two ways: "to have a successful journey" and "to do well in business affairs."

These definitions give us the two main understandings of prospering—prospering in finances and prospering in the affairs of life.

The Hebrew words for prosperity are related to the above two definitions, but with slightly different shades of meaning related to each one. Each of these words is listed with examples so that you can see each one in its context.

In the Scriptures we see the word "prospering" used in many different contexts. Sometimes it is used with regard to kingdoms, but most often it is used in a personal way: prospering in our way, prospering in everything we put our hand to, prospering in our souls, in creation, in spreading cities abroad, in how a war is going, in building walls, in the increase of riches, in sowing seed, in large flocks, in female and male servants, and in camels, donkeys, gold, silver, etc.

The definitions for "prosperity" that I am using here are summarized in *Strong's Exhaustive Concordance of the Bible*, according to the King James Version.

When we look at Strong's definition of the words, let us remember that we can't just choose which word we prefer for the translation. The translators have carefully chosen the definition according to context and other criteria!

Listed below are two definitions—one from the Hebrew and one from the Greek. These definitions are then followed by sample scriptures that use the particular word defined.

(Please note: A complete list of the Hebrew, Aramaic and Greek definitions of "prosperity" can be found in the glossary at the end of the book.)

Strong's Reference No. 6743 (Hebrew)

צָלַח - tsalach

1)   to rush
2)   to advance, prosper, make progress, succeed, be profitable
2a)   to prosper
2b)   to make prosperous, bring to successful issue, cause to prosper
2b2)   to show or experience prosperity, prosper

Sample Scriptures using *tsalach*.

> "The keeper of the prison looked not to any thing that was under his hand; because the LORD was with him,

and that which he did, the LORD made it to *prosper.*"
(Gen. 39:23)

"This book of the law shall not depart out of thy
mouth; but thou shalt meditate therein day and night,
that thou mayest observe to do according to all that
is written therein: for then thou shalt make thy way
prosperous, and then thou shalt have good success."
(Josh. 1:8)

Strong's **Reference No. 2137 (Greek)**

εὐοδόω – **euodoo**

1)   to grant a prosperous and expeditious journey, to
        lead by a direct and easy way
2)   to grant a successful issue, to cause to prosper
3)   to prosper, be successful

All the Scriptures using *euodoo*.

"Making request, if by any means now at length I
might have a prosperous journey by the will of God
to come unto you," (Rom. 1:10)

"Upon the first day of the week let every one of you
lay by him in store, as God hath prospered him, that
there be no gatherings when I come." (1 Cor. 16:2)

"Beloved, I wish above all things that thou mayest
prosper and be in health, even as thy soul prospereth."
(3 John 1:2)

Chapter 2

Prosperity of the Patriarchs

When we study the Bible, it is good to learn how certain things started. By tracing the beginnings of things, we can discern the pattern of God's thoughts.

The patriarchs prospered greatly under the hand of God, yet each one prospered differently. Why was this so?

From the beginning we can see that God's heart was set on blessing mankind. God was pleased with the works of His hands. He saw that what He had made was good. God planted a garden eastward in Eden, then He placed a man in it and gave that man the right to freely eat of all the trees in the Garden, except for the Tree of the Knowledge of Good and Evil.

What a lifestyle Adam had—his job was to dress and keep the Garden, and, as he did so, he could just reach out and take fruit from the trees and eat. There was no lack of anything; there was complete abundance everywhere: "...every tree that is pleasant to the sight, and good for food" (Gen. 2:9b). What a pleasant lifestyle Adam enjoyed, and he could satisfy himself with as much of anything whenever he wanted.

We also see that near Eden there was good gold, bdellium, and the onyx stone. Clearly, Adam had been well provided for.

The First Key to Poverty: Disobedience

But what happened to change this beautiful picture? The prob-lem was that disobedience crept into this idyllic setting. Adam disobeyed God by eating from the Tree of the Knowledge of Good and Evil.

What were the consequences of his choice to do so?

> "And unto Adam he said, Because thou hast hear-kened unto the voice of thy wife, and hast eaten of the tree, of which I commanded thee, saying, Thou shalt not eat of it: *cursed is the ground* for thy sake; *in sor-row shalt thou eat of it all the days of thy life*; Thorns also and thistles shall it bring forth to thee; and thou shalt eat the herb of the field; *In the sweat of thy face* shalt thou eat bread, till thou return unto the ground;" (Gen. 3:17)

Adam had been given a simple command: He was not to eat of the Tree of the Knowledge of Good and Evil, but he disobeyed this command. The greatest mistake mankind can ever make is to disobey God. When Adam listened to his wife, he hearkened unto the serpent and obeyed Satan, thereby disobeying his Creator.

From then on life would no longer be filled with prosperity and abundance for humanity. Rather than cursing the man, however, God cursed the ground: "Thorns also and thistles shall it bring forth to thee; and thou shalt eat the herb of the field; In the sweat of thy face shalt thou eat bread, till thou return unto the ground."

This change in the ground has caused mankind to struggle and strive throughout life for prosperity. The ground would no longer release the blessings easily. Instead, it now produces thorns and thistles, and mankind must sweat in order to reap a harvest from it.

> From Adam we find the first key to poverty: *Disobedience.*

You cannot expect to be blessed by our heavenly Father, if you willingly disobey Him.

Noah

As mankind began to multiply on earth, God saw that the wickedness of man was great, and that every imagination of the thoughts of human hearts was only evil continually. The Lord repented that he had made mankind on the earth, and this all grieved Him deeply within His heart.

The Lord decided that He would destroy man from the earth. (See Gen. 6:5-7.) The Lord destroyed every living substance upon the face of the ground, both man and cattle and creeping things, and even the birds in the heavens. The Great Flood destroyed everyone except for Noah and the ones he took along with him (eight members of his own family and two or seven of every kind of animal life).

Why was Noah given grace so that he and the few others were spared this destruction?

> "These are the generations of Noah: *Noah was a just man and perfect* in his generations, and Noah *walked with God.*" (Gen. 6:9)

> "And Noah did according unto all that the LORD
> commanded him." (Gen. 5:7)

Noah had two things going for him: 1) His character; 2) His actions. Noah was just and perfect in his generations, and he was righteous. Noah walked with God and obeyed Him.

Righteousness and Obedience—Twin Themes of the New Testament

> "Sacrifice and offering, burnt offerings, and offerings for sin You did not desire, nor had pleasure in them" (which are offered according to the law), then He said, *'Behold, I have come to do Your will, O God.'*"He takes away the first that He may establish the second." (Heb. 10:8-9 NKJV).

Jesus came *to do His Father's will.*

Through disobedience, the curse of poverty came into the world; through obedience, we shall see that prosperity is returned to us.

Noah was faithful and He believed God. In believing God, Noah was obedient, and he built the ark which saved himself, his family, and members of the animal kingdom. God blessed Noah for his obedience.

The Second Key to Poverty: Dishonoring One's Parents

In the account of Noah we also see a second key to poverty: Dishonoring one's parents. (See Deut. 5:16.)

> "And Noah began to be an husbandman, and he
> planted a vineyard: And he drank of the wine, and
> was drunken; and he was uncovered within his tent.
> And Ham, the father of Canaan, saw the nakedness
> of his father, *and told* his two brethren without. And
> Shem and Japheth took a garment, and laid it upon
> both their shoulders, and went backward, and covered
> the nakedness of their father; and their faces were
> backward, and they saw not their father's nakedness.
> And Noah awoke from his wine, and knew what his
> younger son had done unto him. And he said, Cursed
> be Canaan; a servant of servants shall he be unto his
> brethren. And he said, Blessed be the LORD God of
> Shem; and Canaan shall be his servant. God shall en-
> large Japheth, and he shall dwell in the tents of Shem;
> and Canaan shall be his servant." (Gen. 9:20-28)

Although it was wrong for Noah to be drunk, it was a dishonor-
able act that his son Ham looked upon his father's nakedness
and then told his brothers. His brothers were righteous in that
they went into the tent backwards and covered their father. Remember, "Love covers a multitude of sins." (See Prov. 10:12
and Prov. 17:9.)

Because Ham dishonored his father, a curse came on his descendants through his son Canaan, who was to be a servant of
servants!

> "Honour thy father and mother; which is the first
> commandment with promise; That it may be well
> with thee, and thou mayest live long on the earth."
> (Eph. 6:2)

Abraham

"Now the LORD had said unto Abram, Get thee out of thy country, and from thy kindred, and from thy father's house, unto a land that I will show thee: And I will make of thee a great nation, and I will bless thee, and make thy name great; and thou shalt be a blessing: And I will bless them that bless thee, and curse him that curseth thee: and in thee shall all families of the earth be blessed. So Abram departed, as the LORD had spoken unto him." (Gen. 12:1-4)

How did the Lord prosper Abraham and why did He do so?

First, the LORD said to Abram, "Get thee out of thy country, and from thy kindred, and from thy father's house unto a land that I will show thee."

The LORD had given Abram a commandment. What was Abram's response? Read verse 4, "So Abram departed as the LORD had spoken unto him."

Abram *obeyed* the LORD. *Obedience* is a very important key to prosperity.

Let us also remember that when Abram obeyed God, he had to leave his home, country, and family.

Obedience is not always an easy thing to do; however, it is always the right thing to do—the absolutely best choice of all.

The apostles made the choice to leave everything and obey. To those who obey, there are precious promises from God. (See Mark 10:28-30.)

The commandment given to Abram was also followed by a promise. In fact, the LORD made a contract with Abram:

> "Get thee out of thy country, and from thy kindred, and from thy father's house, unto a land that I will show thee: And I will make of thee a great nation, and I will bless thee, and make thy name great; and thou shalt be a blessing: And I will bless them that bless thee, and curse him that curseth thee: and in thee shall all families of the earth be blessed" (Gen. 12:1-3).

Did God bless Abram?

We find the answer in Genesis 13:1-2: "And Abram went up out of Egypt, he, and his wife, and all that he had, and Lot with him, into the south. And Abram was *very rich* in cattle, in silver, and in gold."

How blessed was Abram?

Genesis 13:2, 5-6 gives us a clear answer to this question: "And Abram was very rich in cattle, in silver, and in gold... And Lot also, which went with Abram, had flocks, and herds, and tents. And the land was not able to bear them, that they might dwell together: for their substance was great, so that they could not dwell together."

Lot, who was with Abram, was blessed according to the promise of God: "I will bless them that bless thee." The blessing on them was so great that the land was not able to bear them together.

Their substance was so great that they had to depart from one another!

Let us remember that the blessings that came upon Abram were not solely because of the Promise, but they came upon him because he fulfilled the conditions of the Promise. Abram left his country, his kindred, and his family. As a direct result of his obedience, God blessed him.

Clearly, Abram was obedient, and we must be obedient, as well.

In the account of the war that is recorded in Genesis 14, the kings of Sodom and Gomorrah were defeated, and they fled from the scene. The goods and people of the kings were captured and because Lot was living in Sodom at the time, he also was taken captive along with his goods.

When Abram heard of this, he armed his trained servants and pursued and smote them. Abram defeated the four kings, whereas the five kings had been unable to do so! He brought back all the goods and people that were captured, including Lot and his goods.

Abram was a powerful man *because* he was blessed by God.

> "And Melchizedek king of Salem brought forth bread and wine: and he was the priest of the most high God. And he blessed him, and said, *Blessed be Abram of the most high God*, possessor of heaven and earth: And blessed be the most high God, which hath delivered thine enemies into thy hand. And he gave him tithes of all. And the king of Sodom said unto Abram, Give me the persons, and take the goods to thyself. And Abram said to the king of Sodom, I have lift up mine hand unto the LORD, the most high God, the possessor of heaven and earth, That I will not take from a thread even to a shoelatchet, and that *I will not*

take any thing that is thine, lest thou shouldest say, I
have made Abram rich." (Gen. 14:18-23)

After this great battle, Abram humbled himself before Melchizedek, the king of Salem. He humbled himself by giving Melchizedek a tithe of all that he had. A tithe is the tenth part of your
goods (or your earnings). This will be explained more fully in
the chapter on tithes and offerings (Chapter 7).

We learn more about Melchizedek in the Book of Hebrews:

> "For this Melchisedec, king of Salem, priest of the
> most high God, who met Abraham returning from the
> slaughter of the kings, and blessed him; To whom
> also Abraham *gave a tenth part of all*; first being by
> interpretation King of righteousness, and after that
> also King of Salem, which is, King of peace; Without
> father, without mother, without descent, having nei-
> ther beginning of days, nor end of life; but made like
> unto the Son of God; abideth a priest continually."
> (Heb. 7:1-4)

> "So also Christ glorified not himself to be made an
> high priest; but he that said unto him, Thou art my
> Son, today have I begotten thee. As he saith also in
> another place, Thou art a priest for ever after the order
> of Melchisedec." (Heb. 5:5-6)

What did Melchizedek bring to Abram? He brought bread and
the wine to him. When we take the bread and wine during a communion service, we take it in remembrance of Jesus dying on the
cross for us.

This eternal high priest brought that bread and wine and Abram
gave tithes to him. When we give our money to God in the form

of our tithes and offerings, it is really our life that we are bringing to Him. We spend hours and days changing our labor and
time into money. The money represents our life. When Jesus
gave His body and blood, the bread and the wine, He was giving
His life.

This is another key to why Abram prospered: *He honored God*
with his money.

It is interesting to see that Abram would not take the goods that
were offered to him by the King of Sodom, for he did not want
that king to be able to take the credit for making him rich. (See
Gen. 14:21-23.)

Levels of Obedience and Prosperity

Without any doubt, the key to Abraham's prosperity was his
obedience. As he was obedient, God blessed him. It's important
to realize, though, that there are levels to obedience just as there
are levels to prosperity.

In Genesis chapter 22, God decides to test Abraham's obedience. It is easy to obey God when you want to do what He says,
or when the task is simple. Let's read Genesis chapter 22 to see
what God asked Abraham to do.

Abraham was told *to go* to the land of Moriah. He already knew
how to go there, so the directions were not the difficulty that lay
in front of him. To prove Abraham's willingness to sacrifice his
son, Isaac, it was not necessary for Abraham to travel, yet it is
important for us to realize that Abraham had grown in his obedience. God so often likes to grow things; for example, if you
use your "talents" well, you are given more "talents," but if you

don't use what you have, even that will be taken away from you. (See Matt. 25:14-29.)

> "Take now thy son, thine only son Isaac, whom thou lovest, and get thee into the land of Moriah; and offer him there for a burnt offering upon one of the mountains which I will tell thee of." (Gen. 22:2)

Go and witness. Preach the gospel. Teach. Pray. Study the Word. Work. Give. Be persecuted. Be martyred. Can any of these things which we may be asked to do compare with being asked to offer up your only son as a burnt offering?

Because God had given Abraham the promise that a great nation would come from him, the only solution would be that God would have to raise Isaac from the dead. With this great faith Abraham went to slay his son Isaac, but he was interrupted from doing so.

> "By faith Abraham, when he was tried, offered up Isaac: and he that had received the promises offered up his only begotten son. Of whom it was said, That in Isaac shall thy seed be called: Accounting that God was able to raise him up, even from the dead; from whence also he received him in a figure." (Heb. 11:17)

> "By myself have I sworn, saith the LORD, for because thou hast done this thing, and hast not withheld thy son, thine only son: That in blessing I will bless thee, and in multiplying I will multiply thy seed as the stars of the heaven, and as the sand which is upon the sea shore; and thy seed shall possess the gate of his enemies; And in thy seed shall all the nations of the earth be blessed; *because thou hast obeyed my voice.*" (Gen. 22:16-18)

All the blessings that came upon Abraham, the blessings that came upon his descendants, and the blessings that came to all nations were because Abraham believed and obeyed God's voice.

If you want to do anything for God, you must *listen to* and *obey* His voice.

Isaac

> "And God said, Sarah thy wife shall bear thee a son indeed; and thou shalt call his name Isaac: and I will establish my covenant with him for an everlasting covenant, and with his seed after him." (Gen. 17:19)

In Isaac we see a different way of obtaining prosperity. Isaac obtained prosperity through the actions of another person. First, he inherited all the goods that Abraham had. But not only that, he also inherited the covenant that God had made with Abraham.

> "And Abraham gave all that he had unto Isaac." (Gen. 25:5)

> "And the LORD appeared unto him, and said, Go not down into Egypt; dwell in the land which I shall tell thee of: Sojourn in this land, and *I will be with thee, and will bless thee*; for unto thee, and unto thy seed, I will give all these countries, and I will perform the oath which I sware unto Abraham thy father; And I will make thy seed to multiply as the stars of heaven, and will give unto thy seed all these countries; and in thy seed shall all the nations of the earth be blessed; *Because that Abraham obeyed my voice, and kept*

my charge, my commandments, my statutes, and my laws." (Gen. 26:2-5)

Isaac received the blessing because of his father, Abraham. It was not by his own efforts that he was blessed. He received the blessing as an inheritance.

> "Sojourn in this land, and I will be with thee, and will bless thee;" (Gen. 26:3)

> "Then Isaac sowed in that land, and received in the same year an hundredfold: and the LORD blessed him. And the man waxed great, and went forward, and grew until he became very great: For he had possession of flocks, and possession of herds, and great store of servants: and the Philistines envied him." (Gen. 26:12-14)

Because of the death of Jesus, we have inherited the promises that came to Jesus through Abraham and Isaac.

> "And if ye be Christ's, then are ye Abraham's seed, and heirs according to the promise." (Gal. 3:29)

How do we obtain these promises?

> "That ye be not slothful, but followers of them who through faith and patience inherit the promises." (Heb. 6:12)

Through the inheritance and the blessings of God, Isaac became so great that even Abimelech, the king of the Philistines, was afraid of him. They asked him to move away because he was mightier than them. They saw that the Lord was with him and wanted a covenant with him so that Isaac would not harm them! (See Gen. 26.)

Isaac prospered greatly through the grace of *inheritance*, and this is an important key to prosperity.

(Please note that you can only receive the inheritance that was passed from Abraham to Isaac to Jesus if you belong to Christ—Gal. 3:29.)

Jacob

Rebekah had two children in her womb, but even before they were born they were destined by God for different purposes. "Jacob have I loved, but Esau have I hated."

> "When Rebecca also had conceived by one, even by our father Isaac; (For the children being not yet born, neither having done any good or evil, that the purpose of God according to election might stand, not of works, but of him that calleth;) It was said unto her, The elder shall serve the younger. As it is written, Jacob have I loved, but Esau have I hated." (Rom. 9:10-13)

The Scriptures show us very clearly that Jacob was chosen. Why God decided to choose Jacob and not Esau is His own business. But this grace that was given to Jacob and to every believing Christian is a precious gift. Sometimes it is hard to understand, but it in no way takes away the God-given responsibility to preach the Gospel of Jesus Christ to every creature. (See Mark 16:15 in the KJV Bible.)

Having been chosen by God over his elder brother, Esau, Jacob received blessings from his father and from God.

> "And Isaac called Jacob, and blessed him…. And God Almighty bless thee, and make thee fruitful, and multiply thee, that thou mayest be a multitude of people; *And give thee the blessing of Abraham*, to thee, and to thy seed with thee; that thou mayest inherit the land wherein thou art a stranger, which God gave unto Abraham." (Gen. 28:1-4)

> "I am the LORD God of Abraham thy father, and the God of Isaac: the land whereon thou liest, to thee will I give it, and to thy seed; And thy seed shall be as the dust of the earth, and thou shalt spread abroad to the west, and to the east, and to the north, and to the south: and in thee and in thy seed shall all the families of the earth be blessed." (Gen. 28:13-14)

In response to this blessing Jacob promised to give God a tenth of all that was given to him. (See Gen. 28:22 in the KJV Bible.)

So then, having received blessings from his father, Isaac, and from the Lord, Jacob must have had an easy life!?

No. Life was not easy for Jacob. Indeed, he was the holder of the promises that were given to Abraham and Isaac, yet there was quite a long waiting period before he received them.

Jacob agreed to work for his mother's brother, Laban, for seven years in return for Laban's daughter, Rachel. On the wedding night Laban deceived Jacob and brought his other daughter, Leah, to Jacob. (It must have been dark!) After a week he was given Rachel as a wife in return for another seven years of work!

What on earth did Jacob think about this? How many of us would work for seven years for our wives, and then find we have to work another seven years?

Fourteen years!

After those fourteen years, an agreement was reached with La-ban in regard to Jacob's future wage. Jacob would receive from the flocks which he had looked after during the fourteen years. When Jacob started to work for Laban, the flocks were little in number; after the fourteen years, however, there was a multitude of animals. (See Gen. 30:27-33.)

Jacob then worked an additional six years for Laban.

During that time Jacob used his "talent" as a shepherd to build and strengthen his own flocks. Using his experience as a shep-herd, he was able to take control of when the cattle would con-ceive and other matters relating to the cattle and the sheep.

> "And the man *increased exceedingly*, and had much cattle, and maidservants, and menservants, and cam-els, and asses." (Gen. 30:43)

This long period of work for Jacob was not easy. Laban was not a good employer, as was evidenced by him changing Jacob's wages ten times and requiring him to replace damaged and sto-len goods. These would be hard terms for a stranger, let alone for your own son-in-law! He went through drought, frost, and sleeplessness. It was not an easy time. (See Gen. 31:38-42.)

Sometimes, as Christians, we can look at the promises and in-heritance so much that we forget that hard work is sometimes also required. Jacob went through affliction and labor for twenty years! This is why the Scripture says that it is through faith *and patience* that we inherit the promises of God. (See Heb. 6:12.)

The promises are true, but sometimes we have to labor. Do not be surprised.

Hard work is another key to prosperity.

Wrestling With God!

> "And Jacob was left alone; and there wrestled a man with him until the breaking of the day. And when he saw that he prevailed not against him, he touched the hollow of his thigh; and the hollow of Jacob's thigh was out of joint, as he wrestled with him. And he said, Let me go, for the day breaketh. And he said, *I will not let thee go, except thou bless me*. And he said unto him, What is thy name? And he said, Jacob. And he said, Thy name shall be called no more Jacob, but Israel: for as a prince hast thou power with God and with men, and hast prevailed. And Jacob asked him, and said, Tell me, I pray thee, thy name. And he said, Wherefore is it that thou dost ask after my name? *And he blessed him there*." (Gen. 32:24)

Here we see Jacob's attitude toward God. He would not let God go until he was blessed. This attitude pleased God. This reminds me of when the Canaanite woman spoke to Jesus for the healing of her daughter. She was not put off by Jesus' protestations that He would not help. She knew that God would help.

> "And, behold, a woman of Canaan came out of the same coasts, and cried unto him, saying, Have mercy

on me, O Lord, thou son of David; my daughter is grievously vexed with a devil. But he answered her not a word. And his disciples came and besought him, saying, Send her away; for she crieth after us. But he answered and said, I am not sent but unto the lost sheep of the house of Israel. Then came she and worshipped him, saying, Lord, help me. But he answered and said, It is not meet to take the children's bread, and cast it to dogs. And she said, Truth, Lord: yet the dogs eat of the crumbs which fall from their masters' table. Then Jesus answered and said unto her, *O woman, great is thy faith: be it unto thee even as thou wilt. And her daughter was made whole from that very hour.*" (Matt. 15:22-28)

This woman persevered until she received from Jesus what she needed. Jesus acknowledged how great her faith was in light of her determination.

If you truly, truly know that God will bless you, then you will not let Him go. When you don't really believe, then you won't pray much at all.

This attitude of Jacob is described in the Psalms:

"This is the generation of them that seek him, that seek thy face, O Jacob" (Ps. 24:6).

God likes intimacy with us, but He won't force us to come close to Him. We have to desire to draw close to Him and seek His face. Let us have eyes to see. Intimacy with God and prayer to Him are vital keys to prosperity.

Joseph

In Joseph's life we see what appears to be many contradictions. Instead of blessing and prosperity, we see anguish, suffering, toil, and affliction. Surely we should see prosperity, not affliction in his life. Shouldn't we? Well, let's see what the Scriptures have to say about this.

Joseph was born into a prosperous family; his father was Jacob, a man who was mightily blessed by God. Living in the house of a prosperous father, Joseph was blessed through him. Part of that blessing was the receiving of a multi-colored coat that was given to him by his father.

At the age of seventeen, Joseph had two dreams in which it was revealed that his father, mother and his eleven brothers would bow down to him, and that he would rule and have dominion over them. This revelation, along with the fact that his father loved him more than his other children made his brothers envious of Joseph. In fact, one of them actually suggested killing him; eventually the brothers decided to sell him. (See Gen. 37:23-28.)

This stripping away of Joseph's coat of many colors is quite significant. It represented the transition in his life from his rightful position in his family's house as an heir to the position of a common slave with no rights. His covering was stripped away from him.

It is sometimes hard to understand the relationship between our inheritance of prosperity from God and the times when we are called into suffering and poverty.

But as we follow the account of Joseph, we see that his enormous change of circumstances was for a purpose—the saving of the whole world, and we see the outcome that God had put in place for him!

> "God sent me before you to preserve you a posterity in the earth, and to save your lives by a great deliverance. So now it was not you that sent me hither, but God: and he hath made me a father to Pharaoh, and lord of all his house, and a ruler throughout all the land of Egypt." (Gen. 45:7-8)

We can also see this laying aside of our rights in the life of Jesus:

> "Who, being in the form of God, thought it not robbery to be equal with God: *But made himself of no reputation, and took upon him the form of a servant, and was made in the likeness of men*: And being found in fashion as a man, he humbled himself, and became obedient unto death, even the death of the cross." (Phil. 2:6-8)

> "For ye know the grace of our Lord Jesus Christ, that, though he was rich, *yet for your sakes he became poor*, that ye through his poverty might be rich." (2 Cor. 8:9)

As it says in Ecclesiastes, "The end of a matter is better than the beginning" (Eccles. 7:8).

When Jesus, the King of kings and Lord of lords, came to earth, He was stripped of His majesty. For the purposes of God He was obedient unto the death of the cross, and because of His obedience, He was highly exalted, and given a name above all names.

In the continuing account of Joseph's life (see Gen. 39), we see him being trained for the job that was ahead of him. Through difficult times, the *careful positioning* of his circumstances brought him to the fulfillment of his life's purpose: the saving of the world.

First, he was sold into the hands of Potiphar.

Second, he was put in prison, because he would not succumb to the advances of Potiphar's wife.

While he was in prison, the Lord used Joseph to interpret the dreams of Pharaoh's baker and butler.

These interpretations proved to be true, yet the butler forgot Joseph and left him in prison.

If the butler had remembered his promise to help Joseph, then Joseph may have been released and, therefore, he would not have been in the necessary position when Pharaoh received his dreams from God. This forgetfulness of the butler's was part of the purposes of God, and it reveals the importance of timing, which God has set for us and which we need to accept with patience.

Third, Joseph was called before Pharaoh and was ready to interpret Pharaoh's dream and get ready for the work that lay ahead for him. (Pharaoh's dream can be found in Genesis chapter 41.)

I think it is quite poignant that Joseph named his first two children Manasseh and Ephraim.

Manasseh: For God said he hath made me forget all my toil.

Ephraim: For God hath caused me to be fruitful in the land of my affliction.

When you put the meaning of their two names together, we learn: "God has made me forget all my toil and caused me to be fruitful in the land of my affliction." It is quite clear from the account of Joseph's life that it was for the purposes of God that he went through that "land of affliction." It is also quite clear that a season of fruitfulness follows such times.

Each of the patriarchs teaches us a different key to prosperity:

Noah	*Righteousness*
Abraham	*Obedience*
Isaac	*Inheritance*
Jacob	*Hard work*
Joseph	*Sacrifice and suffering*

Chapter 3

Prosperity of the Kings

In our study of prosperity we can look at the kings of Israel and Judah for additional insights. When they listened and served God, He gave them length of days and prosperity. When they did not listen, they perished early.

> "But with kings on the throne he sets them forever, and they are exalted… *If they listen and serve him, they complete their days in prosperity*, and their years in pleasantness. *But if they do not listen, they perish by the sword and die without knowledge.*" (Job 36:7 NASV)

God said to Solomon, "Ask! What shall I give you?" Let's see how Solomon answered.

Solomon offered a thousand burnt offerings on that altar. At Gibeon the LORD appeared to Solomon in a dream by night; and God said, "Ask! What shall I give you?"

And Solomon said: "… *Give to Your servant an understanding heart to judge Your people, that I may discern between good and evil.* For who is able to judge this great people of Yours?" (1 Kings 3:9 NKJV)

"The speech pleased the LORD, that Solomon had asked this thing. Then God said to him: 'Because you have asked this thing, and have not asked long life for yourself, nor have asked riches for yourself, nor have asked the life of your enemies, but have asked for yourself understanding to discern justice, behold, I have done according to your words; see, I have given you a wise and understanding heart, so that there has not been anyone like you before you, nor shall any like you arise after you. And I have also given you what you have not asked: both riches and honour, so that there shall not be anyone like you among the kings all your days." (1 Kings 3:3-14 NKJV)

What better way to start a kingship than to offer a thousand burnt offerings to the Lord?

God's response was, "Ask! What shall I give you?"

What an offer! Almighty God said, "Ask! What shall I give you?"

If many people were given the same offer today, they might respond by saying, "Let me see, hmmm, a new Ferrari, a big house with a swimming pool, a summer home by the lake, trips around the world, etc."

Solomon asked for an understanding heart to judge God's people. Solomon obviously felt the importance of leading Israel and his own inadequacy to do a good job. His response to God was born out of doing the best for God's kingdom. Notice something else—how he referred to himself as "Your servant."

I've learned that God will always respond to our requests for provisions to build His kingdom. Not only did God give Solomon wisdom, but He also gave him what he did not ask for—riches and honor.

The truth of these verses is reflected in 3 John:

"Beloved, I wish above all things that thou mayest prosper and be in health, even as thy soul prospereth" (3 John 1:2).

God desires us to prosper and have a long life. Yet, more important to Him is the prospering of our souls. Solomon showed maturity (the prospering of his soul) in desiring an understanding heart for God's people. Then God responded with riches and honor. If we view being a Christian as a means to gain money, things, and possessions, we are showing great immaturity. If we see prospering as an opportunity for the gospel to advance, then we are getting closer to being the children that God wants.

As we continue to look at the prosperity of the kings of Israel and Judah, we have an opportunity to measure their success. There is a great deal of data in the books of the Kings, especially in regard to the kings' attitudes toward God and the length of their reigns. God said to Solomon,

> "So if you walk in My ways, to keep My statutes and
> My commandments, as your father David walked,
> then I will lengthen your days" (1 Kings 3:14 NKJV).

Apart from the great wealth of David and the immense riches of Solomon, we do not find a great deal with regard to the wealth of the other kings. But, as there is a correlation between God's blessings of wealth and long life, we can look at the length of their reigns to give us an indication of God's response to them.

By making a list of the kings who did evil and the kings who did right, we find an astonishing difference in the relative lengths of their reigns.

The average reign of a king who did right was 30.01 years. The average reign of a king who did evil, on the other hand, was 2.81 years!

One king who at first seemed to be an anomaly was King Manasseh. He did great evil, yet he reigned for fifty-five years. The clue to this is found in another book of the Bible. Second Chronicles 1-18 shows us that after years of evil, King Manasseh repented of his ways by removing the strange gods and idols out of the Temple. This shows us the great mercy of God who endured this man's evil and iniquitous ways and yet forgave him. Such is the translation of the name of Manasseh: "causing to forget." God in His great mercy chose to forget Manasseh's sins.

I did not add King Manasseh's reign to the list of kings I cited above, but if we add the reign of Manasseh to the list of kings who did evil, it barely changes the average figure to 4.74 years. I did not include these kings either: Saul, Solomon, Rehoboam, or Shallum, as it is not clear that they behaved continually evilly or righteously. Saul did not follow the Lord with all of his heart, but he certainly didn't worship other gods either. Solomon is a bit of an enigma, as he built the Temple for the Lord, but he also built houses for the gods of his foreign wives. In Rehoboam's reign the Kingdom of Israel was split in two: Israel and Judah. Solomon's son Rehoboam was foolish and he also sinned, but they also humbled themselves before the Lord. Again, I did not add his seventeen-year reign into either column, but if we add it to those who did evil, then the average would be 5.18 years.

Shallum reigned for one month, but we don't really get to know much about him. He reigned during a time when the kings of Israel did evil, but it does not specifically say that he did.

In light of these truths we can see the benefits of doing righteously and living for God.

The following is a list of the different kings and the lengths of their respective reigns.

Kings That Did Evil

Jehoram	8 years
Jehoiachin	0.25 years
Zachariah	0.5 years
Jehoash	16 years
Jeroboam	41 years
Pekah	20 years
Menahem	10 years
Eliakim, changed to Jehoiakim	11 years
Hoshea	9 years
Amon	2 years
Jehoahaz	0.25 years
Ahaz	10 years
Jehoahaz	17 years
Mattaniah, changed to Zedekiah	11 years
Baasha	24 years
Abijam or Abijah	3 years
Nadab	2 years
Ahaziah	2 years
Jehoram (Joram)	12 years
Ahaziah	1 year
Pekahiah	2 years
Omri	12 years
Jeroboam	22 years
Elah	2 years
Zimri	0.02 years
Ahab	22 years

Kings That Did Righteously

David	40 years
Jehoshaphat	25 years
Jehoash (Joash)	40 years
Jotham	16 years
Josiah	31 years
Amaziah	29 years
Hezekiah	29 years
Azariah (Uzziah)	52 years
Asa	41 years
Jehu	28 years

Below are some interesting verses in reference to the kings' relationships with God. I have not included all of the kings, but only some relevant verses that can help us to understand how God works.

King Saul

Saul had the kingdom torn out of his hand because he did not obey the voice of the Lord. When he needed advice from God and God would not speak to him, he was willing to turn to mediums for spiritual help, even though he had removed them from the land. He was willing to go so far as to remove them, yet he fell into the hypocrisy of finding one when God would not speak to him. It seems as if he valued the spiritual side of life, such as speaking to prophets and fasting, rather than valuing GOD himself. (See 1 Sam. 28:5-20.)

King David

The great King David, after whom I named my son, became great because God was with him. His reign was marked by the various times when he inquired of the Lord. David did not make these inquiries to God in order to receive from Him; on the contrary, David drew close to God in order to obey Him. Saul wanted information and guidance from God, but David wanted an intimate and personal relationship with Him.

> "So David went on and became great, *and the LORD God of hosts was with him.*" (2 Sam. 5:10 NKJV)

> "So *David inquired of the LORD*, saying, 'Shall I go up against the Philistines? Will You deliver them into my hand?' *And the LORD said to David*, 'Go up, for I will doubtless deliver the Philistines into your hand.'" (2 Sam. 5:19 NKJV)

King Jeroboam

In the New Testament, Paul tells us to "set our minds on things above not on things on the earth." (See Col. 3:2.)

Jeroboam tried to solve his political problems and fears by setting up molten calves for the people of Israel to worship, so that they would not go to Jerusalem to worship and therefore be drawn back to King Rehoboam and the Kingdom of Judah.

> "And Jeroboam said in his heart, Now shall the kingdom return to the house of David: If this people go up to do sacrifice in the house of the LORD at Jerusalem, then shall the heart of this people turn again unto

their lord, *even* unto Rehoboam king of Judah, and
they shall kill me, and go again to Rehoboam king of
Judah. Whereupon the king took counsel, and made
two calves of gold, and said unto them, It is too much
for you to go up to Jerusalem: behold thy gods, O Israel, which brought thee up out of the land of Egypt.
And he set the one in Bethel, and the other put he in
Dan. And this thing became a sin: for the people went
to worship before the one, even unto Dan." (1 Kings
12:26-30)

Jeroboam should have inquired of the Lord with regard to how
to solve this problem. The advice he received from his worldly
advisors worked in a way on the earthly plane, but it was so far
from the mark on the heavenly plane.

"Because I exalted you from among the people and
made you leader over My people Israel, and tore the
kingdom away from the house of David and gave it to
you—yet you have not been like My servant David,
who kept My commandments and who followed Me
with all his heart, to do only that which was right in
My sight; you also have done more evil than all who
were before you, and have gone and made for yourself other gods and molten images to provoke Me to
anger, and have cast Me behind your back—therefore
behold, I am bringing calamity on the house of Jeroboam, and will cut off from Jeroboam every male
person, both bond and free in Israel, and I will make a
clean sweep of the house of Jeroboam, as one sweeps
away dung until it is all gone.'" (1 Kings 14:7-10
NASV)

Unlike King David, Jeroboam was earthly minded, and he lost
everything for himself and his family.

King Rehoboam

Rehoboam's reign is marked by the exchange of the gold shields for bronze shields. This reveals a fading of the glory.

Under David and Solomon the Kingdom of Israel was a glorious kingdom, but then it began to fade. In fact, it was split into two, with Israel under Jeroboam and Judah under Rehoboam. Yet, in Rehoboam's reign we see the glory fading away.

Why was the glory fading away? What can we learn from Rehoboam's relationship with God that has caused this fading away, and what can we learn from the fading away, as well?

> "Now it happened in the fifth year of King Rehoboam, that Shishak the king of Egypt came up against Jerusalem. He took away the treasures of the house of the LORD and the treasures of the king's house, and he took everything, even taking *all the shields of gold* which Solomon had made. So King Rehoboam *made shields of bronze* in their place." (1 Kings 14:25-27 NASB)

> "Then came Shemaiah the prophet to Rehoboam... Thus saith the LORD, *Ye have forsaken me*, and therefore have I also left you in the hand of Shishak." (2 Chron. 12:5)

If we start to rest on our laurels, we may see the glory fade away. It may start as a little less prayer, fewer quiet times, or not seeking the Lord as much as we used to. It is quite easy to fade away. We can see from Rehoboam's life (in 2 Chron. 12:14) that he did evil because he was not prepared to seek the Lord. That was the start for him; it was an absence of preparation because his life had now been established. Unlike his grandfather David who was always seeking the Lord, Rehoboam stopped doing so and was then humbled by Shishak, the King of Egypt. When we stop seeking God, stop reading His law (His Word), then we find a law that says that evil is always present and waiting at the door. The absence of God will always allow the opportunity for the presence of evil. We can also see from Rehoboam's life that he humbled himself and repented after God sent his prophet to him; we also see that God relented and did not destroy them. So there is always hope! Let us make sure that we also humble ourselves and repent, so God can change our glory from bronze to gold again.

Sin needs to be repented of. Remember, all people have sinned and fallen short of the glory of God. (See Rom. 3:23.) The glory in our lives is the Presence of God within us radiating out from us. Let that radiance be gold, not bronze.

> "So king Rehoboam strengthened himself in Jerusalem, and reigned.... And he did evil, because he prepared not his heart to seek the LORD." (2 Chron. 12:13-14)

From the Scriptures above we can see that when Rehoboam's kingdom was established, it was then that he forsook the law of the LORD, with the result that he sinned; then God allowed the King of Egypt to come against him.

God has many friends when people are trying to establish themselves in Him. How frequent are their prayers at this time. Yet, when many people are established, they find themselves in a comfort zone. It seems that their comfort zone tests their hearts. In light of this, what are we going to do when we are successful?

> "And it came to pass, *when Rehoboam had estab-lished the kingdom*, and had strengthened himself, *he forsook the law of the LORD*, and all Israel with him. And it came to pass, *that* in the fifth year of king Rehoboam Shishak king of Egypt came up against Jerusalem, *because they had transgressed against the LORD*." (2 Chron. 12:1-2)

King Hezekiah

In the life of King Hezekiah we have a wonderful example of how God blesses us. Hezekiah cleaved, departed not, followed, and kept God's commandments. As a result, the LORD was with him and he prospered wherever he went.

> "...he did that which was right in the sight of the LORD, according to all that David his father did.... He trusted in the LORD God of Israel; so that after him was none like him among all the kings of Ju-dah, nor any that were before him. For he clave to the LORD, and departed not from following him, but kept his commandments, which the LORD com-manded Moses. *And the LORD was with him; and he prospered whithersoever he went forth*." (2 Kings 18:3-7)

King Asa

King Asa built and prospered while he was seeking God with all his heart. Therefore, he experienced an incredible victory against the Ethiopians.

> "Asa did what was good and right in the eyes of the
> LORD his God, ... And Asa cried out to the LORD his
> God, and said, 'LORD, it is nothing for You to help,
> whether with many or with those who have no power;
> help us, O LORD our God, for we rest on You, and
> in Your name we go against this multitude. O LORD,
> You are our God; do not let man prevail against You!'
> *So the LORD struck the Ethiopians before Asa and
> Judah,"* (2 Chron. 14:2-12 NKJV)

Although Asa did not go over to other gods, he did start relying more on men than he did on God. He relied on Ben-Hadad of Syria for deliverance, and he relied on physicians to cure his diseased feet. The outcome of these changes was that the Prophet Hanani gave this word: "From now on you shall have wars."

> *"Because you have relied on the king of Syria, and
> have not relied on the LORD your God, therefore
> the army of the king of Syria has escaped from your
> hand.... In this you have done foolishly; therefore
> from now on you shall have wars....* Asa became dis-
> eased in his feet, and his malady was severe; yet *in his
> disease he did not seek the LORD, but the physicians.*
> So Asa rested with his fathers." (2 Chron.16:7-14
> NKJV)

When Asa sought the Lord with all his heart, he was given peace; in that God-given peace he was able to build. However, when Asa sought help from men, he was given wars. In war it is hard to build because all of your attention must go to the battles.

If we look at plants and animals, we can see that they start small (as a tiny seed) and then they begin to grow.

Let us examine our lives. Are we growing, prospering, and building? Or are we continually fighting problems (wars)? Are we moving ahead, or are we going nowhere?

King David was continually seeking the Lord. He ran his race and won. If you have gotten off track by distractions, this is a good time to repent and seek the Lord's face.

King Jehoshaphat

Jehoshaphat sought God as David his forefather had done. Because he did so, God was with him, he had peace, and he was able to build. He became increasingly powerful with great riches and honor. Even his enemies gave tribute to him.

> "Now the LORD was with Jehoshaphat... *Therefore the LORD established the kingdom in his hand*; and all Judah gave presents to Jehoshaphat, and he had riches and honor in abundance. And his heart took delight in the ways of the LORD... And the fear of the LORD fell on all the kingdoms of the lands that were around Judah, so that they did not make war against Jehoshaphat. Also some of the Philistines brought Jehoshaphat presents and silver as tribute." (2 Chron. 17:3-12 NKJV)

The only blemish that can be found in Jehospaphats' reign was that he joined with Ahaziah, King of Israel, for a business venture. They built a fleet of ships to go trading to Tarshish. But God destroyed them. (See 2 Chron. 20:35-37.)

> "Do not be unequally yoked with unbelievers. For what partnership has righteousness with lawlessness?

Or what fellowship has light with darkness?" (2 Cor. 6:14 ESV)

Traditionally we use this verse in reference to marriage to unbelievers. But equally I think we have to be just as careful about being joined to unbelievers in business ventures. How can two walk together unless they be agreed? (See Amos 3:3.)

King Jehoram (of Judah)

Because of his wife, Jehoram joined in the harlotry of King Ahab of Israel, which involved the worship of the Baals. The effect on his life and the people of Judah was immediate. All the good work of his father was destroyed. Edom and Libnah revolted. They were invaded by the Philistines and the Arabians and their wealth was taken away from them. Then he was given an incurable disease, and in severe pain he died and was buried without honor.

> "Jehoram was thirty-two years old when he became king, and he reigned eight years in Jerusalem. And he walked in the way of the kings of Israel, just as the house of Ahab had done, *for he had the daughter of Ahab as a wife*; and he did evil in the sight of the LORD. … After all this the LORD struck him in his intestines with an incurable disease. Then it happened in the course of time, after the end of two years, that his intestines came out because of his sickness; so he died in severe pain." (2 Chron. 21:4-19 NKJV)

From Jehoshapat to Jehoram, how could there be so much change in one generation?

"Do not be unequally yoked with unbelievers. For what partnership has righteousness with lawlessness? Or what fellowship has light with darkness?" (2 Cor. 6:14 ESV)

King Uzziah

"Sixteen years old was Uzziah when he began to reign, and he reigned fifty and two years in Jerusalem.... And he did that which was right in the sight of the LORD... And he sought God in the days of Zechariah... *and as long as he sought the LORD, God made him to prosper.*" (2 Chron. 26:5)

The understanding we gain from looking at all the relationships these kings had with God can be summed up as follows:

". . . as long as he sought the LORD, God made him to prosper" (2 Chron. 26:5).

Chapter 4

Money

The love of money is the root of all evil, according to what the apostle Paul wrote to Timothy. This has often been misquoted as, "Money is the root of all evil." The actual quote is found in Paul's first letter to Timothy:

> "For *the love* of money is the root of all evil" (1 Tim. 6:10).

Yes, it is the love of the money which is the root of all evil, not the money itself. If money were the root of all evil, we could say that God was evil in giving money to Abraham, Isaac, Jacob, Joseph, Solomon, etc. God is never the author of evil, though. So of course money is not evil. But what is money?

What Is Money?

From Genesis we see that the word translated as "money" is כֶּסֶף ,pronounced *keceph,* which means "*silver.*" In conjunction with the word for silver or gold, we have the words gerahs, shekels, and talents, which were used as measurements of weight, thus giving an exact measurement of worth. The money could be a shekel of silver or a shekel of gold, etc. The value was in the amount of gold or silver that was used to make the coin.

We see, then, that with accurate measurements of weight and value, goods and services could be bought and sold for these coins, thereby providing a commercial standard to work with.

As civilization advanced, the value of money changed from the value of the coins themselves to paper money and metal coins, with the value being shown as a promise from the issuing body.

For example, English paper money has a promise from the Bank of England to pay the bearer on demand the number of pounds stated on the note. This is signed by the Chief Cashier ". . . for the Governor and Company of the Bank of England." The value of the note is more than the paper it is printed on; the value is in the power of the promise from the Bank of England.

It is interesting to read what Jesus said when He was questioned about whether people should pay tribute unto Caesar or not:

> They asked, "Is it lawful for us to give tribute unto Caesar, or no? But he perceived their craftiness, and said unto them, Why tempt ye me? Show me a penny. Whose image and superscription hath it? They answered and said, Caesar's. And he said unto them, Render therefore unto Caesar the things which be Caesar's, and unto God the things which be God's" (Luke 20:22).

The coin translated as "a penny" was a Roman *denarius*, Jesus recognized that this piece of money was Caesar's. The power given in the money had come from Caesar.

With all modern currencies the power invested in them can be traced back to their originators. This is why we get fluctuations in currency prices as the powers behind the notes change! We see differences between strong currencies and weak currencies. Currency from Western countries, such as U.S. dollars and UK pounds sterling do not change a great deal in value unless economic conditions warrant such changes. However, currencies from third-world countries and countries at war can fluctuate greatly. These currencies can even end up with no value at all! This is because the value of these currencies is in the power and promises behind them.

In this time we are seeing the representation of the power invested in money being registered more and more in electronic form. Money is moved from one account to another electronically through computers. Often, physical money is not exchanged, because goods are paid for electronically through credit cards.

Even so, the money still represents the power that is behind it. This is true whether it is held in pounds sterling, U.S. dollars, or any other standard.

If there is a complete financial collapse these currencies and the power behind them could be worth nothing. They would only be worth the paper they are written on. *It is well worth having a proportion of your financial worth in hard assets like gold and silver.*

We know from the Book of Revelation that there will come a time when people will not be able to buy or sell without the name or mark or number of the beast. (See Rev. 13:17.)

Let us not forget that this is not determined by how the money is transmitted, physically, electronically, etc., but it is a reflection of the power and authority of the beast behind that particular type of money. Eternal damnation follows those who enter into that system. This will not be something that people will fall into by mistake! Let's make sure that we invest our money into the bank accounts of the Kingdom of Heaven, where moth, rust, and thieves cannot corrupt and steal.

Chapter 5

The Bank of God—Our Bank Account

The Scriptures show us clearly that God has a different view of our finances than we have. For example, the Book of Revelation talks about those who are rich, yet are poor, and those who are poor, yet are rich. (See Rev. 2:9 and 3:17.) These passages suggest that the earthly view of our bank accounts may not be our correct financial position. We may think we are rich, but the truth could be that we are poor, and vice-versa.

The apostle Paul goes so far as to suggest that we indeed have an account:

> "Now you Philippians know also that in the beginning of the gospel, when I departed from Macedonia, no church shared with me concerning giving and receiving but you only. For even in Thessalonica you sent aid once and again for my necessities. Not that I seek the gift, but *I seek the fruit that abounds to your account*" (Phil. 4:15 NKJV).

Paul is saying that because the Philippians gave to him, there is a natural response to the giving—fruit which abounds to their accounts.

Paul recognized that we had an account, but what did Jesus say about it?

> "Do not lay up for yourselves treasures on earth, where moth and rust destroy and where thieves break in and steal; but lay up for yourselves treasures in heaven, where neither moth nor rust destroys and where thieves do not break in and steal. For where your treasure is, there your heart will be also." (Matt. 6:19 NKJV)

So how do we get money or treasure into our account in Heaven?

Jesus gives us a very clear answer to this question:

> "Give, and it will be given to you: good measure, pressed down, shaken together, and running over will be put into your bosom. For with the same measure that you use, it will be measured back to you" (Luke 6:38 NKJV).

As we give, it will be given back to us. It seems that God has set in order spiritual laws that prosper us when we give. O what beautiful wisdom—growth through giving; there is no room for greed in this system. A greedy man would not ever be able to give in faith.

See how this is backed up in 3 John:

> "Beloved, I wish above all things that thou mayest prosper and be in health, even as thy soul prospereth" (3 John 1:2).

Even as thy soul prospereth. As the child of God learns to give, the child of God prospers.

This prosperity comes in proportion to one's spiritual maturity.

We now see why Jesus told the rich young man to give his money away. It is because he had no money in his bank account in Heaven! In fact, he had a lack!

> "So when Jesus heard these things, He said to him, *'You still lack* one thing. Sell all that you have and distribute to the poor, and you will have treasure in heaven; and come, follow Me.' But when he heard this, he became very sorrowful, for he was very rich. And when Jesus saw that he became very sorrowful, He said, 'How hard it is for those who have riches to enter the kingdom of God!'" (Luke 18:22-24 NKJV)

It is important for us not to look on the outside of a person. Though the rich young man was wealthy in the physical realm, he was not spiritually prosperous. It is better to be both!

> "And to the angel of the church of the Laodiceans write, 'These things says the Amen, the Faithful and True Witness, the Beginning of the creation of God: 'I know your works, that you are neither cold nor hot. I could wish you were cold or hot. So then, because you are lukewarm, and neither cold nor hot, I will vomit you out of My mouth. Because you say, *"I am rich, have become wealthy, and have need of nothing"; and do not know that you are wretched, miserable, poor, blind, and naked.'"* (Rev. 3:14-17 NKJV)

Sometimes we are not able to recognize our own spiritual state.

> "And to the angel of the church in Smyrna write, 'These things says the First and the Last, who was dead, and came to life: "I know your works, tribulation, and poverty (but you are rich)."'" (Rev. 2:8-9 NKJV)

You may say that when Jesus was telling the rich young man to give away his money and that he would be rewarded in Heaven that He was teaching that he would receive his reward when he died and went to Heaven!

This is a clearly wrong point of view, because if we continue reading in Luke, we find that Jesus says that His followers would receive both in this present time *and* in the age to come!

> "Then Peter said, 'See, we have left all and followed You.' So He said to them, 'Assuredly, I say to you, there is no one who has left house or parents or brothers or wife or children, for the sake of the kingdom of God, who shall not receive many times more in this present time, and in the age to come eternal life." (Luke 18:28-30 NKJV)

So we can see that in order to increase the amount of money in our heavenly account, we have to give it away.

There is a further aspect to this: if we sow sparingly, we shall reap sparingly, and if we sow bountifully, we shall reap bountifully.

> "But this I say, He which soweth sparingly shall reap also sparingly; and he which soweth bountifully shall reap also bountifully." (2 Cor. 9:6)

What if I don't want to reap bountifully; what if I only want enough to meet my needs?

Believe it or not, that is a selfish response, for *the reason to reap bountifully is so we can have sufficiency to meet every good work!* Who will feed the poor, who will pay for Bibles, churches, Christian radio and TV stations; who will provide for the needs of missionaries and the mission field?

If we receive according to what we give isn't that easier for the people who have more?

There are some who think it is only for the wealthy to give and not for the poor to give. That these laws are only for those who have some of this world's wealth.

> "Now Jesus sat opposite the treasury and saw how the people put money into the treasury. And many who were rich put in much. Then one poor widow came and threw in two mites, which make a quadrans. So He called His disciples to Himself and said to them, 'Assuredly, I say to you that this poor widow has put in more than all those who have given to the treasury; for they all put in out of their abundance, but *she out of her poverty put in all that she had, her whole livelihood.* '" (Mark 41-44 NKJV)

We see here that although the poor widow only put in two mites, Jesus said she had put in more than all the rich people. With God, it is always according to what we have, not according to what we do not have. Also, when we are faithful with little, we shall be faithful with much.

So if we have an account in Heaven, then how do we make withdrawals?

"Cast your bread upon the waters, For you will find it after many days. Give a serving to seven, and also to eight, for you do not know what evil will be on the earth. *If the clouds are full of rain, they empty themselves upon the earth*; And if a tree falls to the south or the north, In the place where the tree falls, there it shall lie." (Eccles. 11:1-3 NKJV)

Solomon said that we should cast our bread on the waters and give a serving to seven and eight. He is not telling us to toss our dinner in the river! Nor is he advising us to give lots of dinner parties.

Instead, he is telling us to *give*. By giving you are ensuring your future, no matter what evil may occur. "If the clouds are full of rain, they empty themselves upon the Earth."

The clouds are in the heavens. When you give your tithes and offerings, or when you give to the poor, you are filling that cloud in Heaven with rain. Clouds full of water empty back down to the Earth. You may not know when, but they most certainly will. My own testimony about tithing proves this: in one day I had a downpour of £100,000 after earning only £2,500 during the entire year before!

"If the clouds are full of rain, they empty themselves upon the earth; and if a tree falls to the south or the north, In the place where the tree falls, there it shall lie." (Eccles. 11:3 NKJV)

When a tree falls to the ground, it remains where it lies because of the weight of the tree and the force of gravity. Through this image God wants us to know that the spiritual laws of receiving after giving are as strong as the universal law of gravity.

Let us now go back to Philippians 4.

> "For even in Thessalonica you sent aid once and again
> for my necessities. Not that I seek the gift, but *I seek
> the fruit that abounds to your account.* Indeed I have
> all and abound. I am full, having received from Ep-
> aphroditus the things sent from you, a sweet-smelling
> aroma, an acceptable sacrifice, well pleasing to God.
> *And my God shall supply all your need according to
> His riches in glory by Christ Jesus.*" (Phil. 4:16-19
> NKJV)

Here we see a dilemma that pastors often have to face. They
want their churches to prosper by giving, yet they do not want to
be seen as seeking the gift. (See Phil. 4:17.)

We have to get rid of pride and preach the Word, even if it seems
to benefit us!

"My God shall supply all your need according to His riches in
glory by Christ Jesus." (Phil. 4:19)

This verse is so often abused and spoken out of context. The
reason Paul could so confidently pronounce that God was going
to supply all their need according to His riches in glory by Christ
Jesus, was because they had just given once and again to him!

Don't think that you will obtain these things from God just by
speaking the verse. It does not come by simply confessing the
verse; first, you have to give! This is exactly what the Philippians had done.

> "He who has pity on the poor lends to the LORD, And
> He will pay back what he has given." (Prov. 19:17
> NKJV)

God is Keeping an Account!

God is aware when we don't use the gold and silver He has given to us. Remember that not everything that has been given to you is for your own use. It may be for another member of the Body of Christ. By holding it back you could be hurting yourself.

> "Your gold and silver is cankered; and the rust of them shall be a witness against you, and shall eat your flesh as it were fire. Ye have heaped treasure together for the last days." (James 5:3)

If you don't use your money for tithes and offerings, God will be aware of it.

> "Will a man rob God? Yet ye have robbed me. But ye say, Wherein have we robbed thee? In tithes and offerings. *Ye are cursed with a curse: for ye have robbed me*, even this whole nation. Bring ye all the tithes into the storehouse, that there may be meat in mine house, and prove me now herewith, saith the LORD of hosts, if I will not open you the windows of heaven, and pour you out a blessing, that there shall not be room enough to receive it. And I will rebuke the devourer for your sakes, and he shall not destroy the fruits of your ground; neither shall your vine cast her fruit before the time in the field, saith the LORD of hosts. And all nations shall call you blessed: for ye shall be a delightsome land, saith the LORD of hosts." (Mal. 3:8-12)

Make sure that you are prospering for God's kingdom and not just collecting for someone who will do good.

"For God gives wisdom and knowledge and joy to a
man who is good in His sight; but to the sinner He
gives the work of gathering and collecting, that he
may give to him who is good before God. This also
is vanity and grasping for the wind." (Eccles. 2:26
NKJV)

As we work for God and disperse His wealth, we can also enjoy
the benefits of that prosperity.

"Here is what I have seen: It is good and fitting for
one to eat and drink, and to enjoy the good of all his
labor in which he toils under the sun all the days of
his life which God gives him; for it is his heritage.
As for every man to whom God has given riches and
wealth, and given him power to eat of it, to receive
his heritage and rejoice in his labor; this is the gift of
God." (Eccles. 5:18-19 NKJV)

Chapter 6

How Do We Obtain Prosperity?

God has put His wisdom into the Bible. Therefore, it's important to know what the Bible has to say about obtaining prosperity.

> "Only be thou strong and very courageous, *that thou mayest observe to do* according to all the law, which Moses my servant commanded thee: turn not from it to the right hand or to the left, *that* thou mayest prosper whithersoever thou goest. This book of the law shall not depart out of thy mouth; but thou shalt meditate therein day and night, *that thou mayest observe to do* according to all that is written therein: for then *thou shalt make thy way prosperous*, and then thou shalt have good success." (Josh. 1:7-8)

God instructed Joshua to be strong and very courageous, that he would observe to do according to all the Law, which Moses commanded.

It is important for us to be strong and very courageous. The Bible will often tell us to do something that requires courage from us. For example, are we willing to tithe when our finances are looking bleak? Or do we lean on our own understanding instead? God is looking for a people who will obey His Word without moving to the right hand or to the left. Can we accept the fact that He always knows what's best? If we observe to do according to all that is in the Bible, then we will prosper wherever we go. But as James said, we must be doers of the Word and not just listeners. It is the application of the Word that will help, not just the reading of it.

So that Joshua could make sure he understood the Law in order to obey it, he was instructed not to let the Law depart out of his mouth and he was commanded to meditate upon it day and night.

Now let us look at Psalm 1. Here is another passage that gives clear instructions to meditate in God's law both day and night.

> "*Blessed* is the man Who walks not in the counsel of the ungodly, Nor stands in the path of sinners, Nor sits in the seat of the scornful; But his delight is in the law of the LORD, *And in His law he meditates day and night.* He shall be like a tree planted by the rivers of water, that brings forth its fruit in its season, whose leaf also shall not wither; and *whatever he does shall prosper.*" (Ps. 1:1-3 NKJV)

The reading of God's Word should be like book ends holding the hours of each day. We should give our attention to it the first thing in the morning and the last thing at night.

To read the Bible through once each year requires you to read only eighty-five verses a day. These verses can be read in as little as twenty to forty minutes. Reading the Bible once a year should be an absolute minimum for anyone who wants to live a life of godliness and be able to teach His Word.

There are many things God wants to teach His people, but:

> "We have much to say, and hard to explain, since you have become dull of hearing. For though by this time you ought to be teachers, you need someone to teach you again the first principles of the oracles of God; and you have come to need milk and not solid food" (Heb. 5:11-12 NKJV).

We need to take seriously the admonition to study the Word, so that we may be approved by God:

> "Study to shew thyself approved unto God, a workman that needeth not to be ashamed, rightly dividing the word of truth" (2 Tim. 2:15).

> "Finally God told Joshua to "observe to do according to all that is written therein: for then *thou* shalt make thy way prosperous, and then *thou* shalt have good success" (Josh. 1:8).

When we observe to do according to all that is written in the Word, when we scrutinize and inspect our lives to see that we are doing all that is written in the Bible, then *we* make our way prosperous, and *we* will have good success.

God does *not* promise to make us prosperous. Notice that it is *ourselves* that make our way prosperous! When we *do* the things that are commanded to us in the Bible!

I cannot overemphasize the fact that it is not God who prospers us; it is ourselves who prosper ourselves, *if* we obey what God commands us to do in the Bible.

Seeking the Lord

"Sixteen years old was Uzziah when he began to reign, and he reigned fifty and two years in Jerusalem.... And he did that which was right in the sight of the LORD... And he sought God in the days of Zechariah... *and as long as he sought the LORD, God made him to prosper.*" (2 Chron. 26:3-5)

This is something we see over and over again in the Old Testament. The kings of Israel and Judah who chose to seek God always prospered. On the other hand, those who did evil and did not seek the LORD, would see a decline. (See the chapter on Kings.)

God prospers His servants because they want to serve. You cannot build the Kingdom of God unless you are a servant. You cannot be a servant unless you listen. Unless you seek God in order to listen to His instructions, you will not hear. If you do not hear, how can you obey?

Consider the problems Joshua had at the city of Ai and with the Gibeonites. Both of these problems would have been avoided if he had sought the Lord *before* the events.
(See Josh. 7, 8, and 9.)

King David was always inquiring of the Lord. He was always seeking Him. His inquiring and seeking saved him a great deal of trouble. (See 1 Sam. 23:1-13.)

Giving

If you want to prosper as a Christian, you must have a soul that gives willingly. We need to be rich towards God, rich towards the poor, and rich in every good work.

I have heard people say that they only want enough to meet their own needs. Can you see how outrageously selfish this is? Only enough for themselves!

Who is going to provide money for the Church, for the poor, for every good work God wants to do through us?

We know from Joshua 1:7-8 that we need to observe to do according to all that is written in the Law. But what does the Bible say about prospering?

> "Give, and it shall be given unto you; good measure, pressed down, and shaken together, and running over, shall men give into your bosom. For with the same measure that ye mete withal it shall be measured to you again." (Luke 6:38)

So here again we see the wonders of the wisdom of God. He has decided to prosper His children when they give! What an incredible law.

Every caring father wants to increase the prosperity of his children and wants them to be generous, which would be their safeguard against greed. In the same way God has set a law that prospers His children as they give.

Isn't that amazing, especially when you consider the fact that giving and greed are opposites.

> "Beloved, I wish above all things that thou mayest
> prosper and be in health, *even* as thy soul prospereth."
> (3 John 1:2)

As our soul prospers, as we learn to give, God prospers us in direct proportion to our giving.

The same measure we use is measured to us.

Have you ever noticed the structure of Luke 6:38? On the one side we have "give" and on the other "given to you," "good measure," "pressed down," "shaken together," "running over," and "shall men give into your bosom."

This is somewhat similar to a farmer sowing seed. You don't receive just one seed back for each seed sown. Sometimes it is thirty-fold, sixty-fold even one hundred-fold!

God loves to give. Jesus told us that unless a grain of wheat falls into the ground and dies, it remains alone, but if it dies, it bears much fruit. (See John 12:24.)

> "For God so loved the world, that he *gave* his only
> begotten Son, that whosoever believeth in him should
> not perish, but have everlasting life." (John 3:16)

Who should we give to?

We should give our tithes* and offerings* to the church we attend.* (See the chapter on tithes and offerings.)

We should give to the poor and needy.

We should give to good works such as Christian television, radio, evangelism, missionary work, hospitals, secular charities, the blind, etc.

God Gives

Sometimes you hear people say, "O God, if you give me a million dollars I will build you a hospital," or something similar.

What I would say to them in response is: "What are you doing with your $10 or your $100?"

If you are not giving with the little you have, you will never give when you have much more.

> "One who is faithful in a very little is also faithful in much, and one who is dishonest in a very little is also dishonest in much." (Luke 16:10 ESV)

The widow who put her two mites into the treasury gave more than the rich people, because she gave according to what she had—she gave everything!

If you want to grow in prosperity, then grow in giving.

Do we believe what we preach and what we hear?

When I was a fairly new convert and a student, my pastor told me that I did not need to tithe, as I did not have very much money. My response even back then was, "Don't you want me to prosper?"

We can't preach that we prosper through giving and then tell the poor not to give! As a Church, we should encourage the poor to give, while not forgetting our obligation to them at the same time.

Let us see how God provided for Elijah (and the widow):

> "Then the word of the LORD came to him, saying, "Arise, go to Zarephath, which belongs to Sidon, and dwell there. See, I have commanded a widow there to provide for you." So he arose and went to Zarephath. And when he came to the gate of the city, indeed a widow was there gathering sticks. And he called to her and said, "Please bring me a little water in a cup, that I may drink." And as she was going to get it, he called to her and said, "Please bring me a morsel of bread in your hand." So she said, "As the LORD your God lives, I do not have bread, only a handful of flour in a bin, and a little oil in a jar; and see, I am gathering a couple of sticks that I may go in and prepare it for myself and my son, that we may eat it, and die." And Elijah said to her, "*Do not fear*; go and do as you have said, *but make me a small cake from it first, and bring it to me*; and *afterward* make some for yourself and your son. For thus says the LORD God of Israel: 'The bin of flour shall not be used up, nor shall the jar of oil run dry, until the day the LORD sends rain on the earth.'" So she went away and did according to the word of Elijah; and she and he and her household ate for many days. The bin of flour was not used up, nor did the jar of oil run dry, according to the word of the LORD which He spoke by Elijah" (1 Kings 17:8-16 NKJV).

The widow had to *first* give to Elijah and *then* God provided the miracle for her and her household.

It is better to teach and preach giving and prosperity than to foster a climate of dependency, notwithstanding our financial obligations.

Jesus became poor so that we could become rich. This was not just for those who have plenty to give, but for us all—from the poorest to the richest, without partiality.

Remember, He loves us all.

The Wisdom of Solomon

What does Solomon have to say about giving?

> "*Cast your bread* upon the waters, For you will find it after many days. *Give a serving to seven*, and also to eight, For you do not know what evil will be on the earth. If the clouds are full of rain, they empty themselves upon the earth; And if a tree falls to the south or the north, in the place where the tree falls, there it shall lie. He who observes the wind will not sow, And he who regards the clouds will not reap. As you do not know what is the way of the wind, or how the bones grow in the womb of her who is with child, so you do not know the works of God who makes everything. *In the morning sow your seed, and in the evening do not withhold your hand*; for you do not know which will prosper, either this or that, or whether both alike will be good." (Eccles. 11:1-6 NKJV)

1. Cast your bread upon the waters, for you will find it after many days.

Is Solomon really talking about finding soggy bread? No, he means that we need to cast away from ourselves. Give, and you will get it back after a period of time. This is a confirmation of Luke 6:38, and this is a bit like feeding ducks. Throw your bread out, and in this way you will be feeding others. Don't worry; you will receive a reward after a period of time passes.

2. Give a serving to seven and also to eight, for you do not know what evil will be on the Earth.

Again, we are admonished to GIVE. This may mean that we should invite more people over for meals, especially those who cannot repay you. Develop a strategy that will lead to increase. Give to seven, to eight, then nine and ten. You do not know what will happen at any given time; you may suddenly be called to Heaven, or you may suddenly lose all your money. But if you have a good account* in Heaven, you will be all right. (See the chapter on your bank account.)

3. If the clouds are full of rain, they empty themselves upon the Earth; and if a tree falls to the south or the north, in the place where the tree falls, there it shall lie.

Where are the clouds? They are in the heavens where the birds fly. When Jesus said to the rich young man to give his money away to the poor, and that he would then have treasure in Heaven, *He did not say that he could not receive withdrawals* from his heavenly bank account!!

When your heavenly bank accounts (clouds) are full of giving (rain), they empty themselves upon the Earth. This is a law—a spiritual law. To confirm this law to us, we are told that if a tree falls to the south or the north, in the place where the tree falls, there it shall lie. What is Solomon talking about? He is talking about forces. What causes the tree to fall and remain where it falls? It is a great force, one of the principles of physics—the law of gravity.

To confirm to us the spiritual law of giving and receiving back to Earth, God has chosen to compare it with the *universal* law of gravity. It is always in force, and it never changes.

Think about it.

More Verses on How to Prosper

"Pray for the peace of Jerusalem: they shall prosper that love thee." (Ps. 122:6)

Here we see the principle of working and giving.

"In the morning sow thy seed, and in the evening withhold not thine hand: for thou knowest not whether shall prosper, either this or that, or whether they both shall be alike good." (Eccles. 11:6)

In Proverbs chapter 8 Solomon talks about the importance of gaining wisdom.

"Riches and honour are with me; yea, durable riches and righteousness. My fruit is better than gold, yea, than fine gold; and my revenue than choice silver. I lead in the way of righteousness, in the midst of the paths of judgment: That I may cause those that love me to inherit substance; and I will fill their treasures." (Prov. 8:18-21)

Solomon also confirms what we learned from the patriarchs that hard work is sometimes needed.

"He becometh poor that dealeth with a slack hand: but the hand of the diligent maketh rich." (Prov. 10:4)

"By humility and the fear of the LORD are riches, and honour, and life." (Prov. 22:4)

"Lay not up for yourselves treasures upon earth, where moth and rust doth corrupt, and where thieves break through and steal: But lay up for yourselves treasures in heaven, where neither moth nor rust doth corrupt, and where thieves do not break through nor steal: *For where your treasure is, there will your heart be also.*" (Matt. 6:19-21)

"Fear not, little flock; for it is your Father's good pleasure to give you the kingdom. Sell that ye have, and give alms; provide yourselves bags which wax not old, a treasure in the heavens that faileth not, where no thief approacheth, neither moth corrupteth. *For where your treasure is, there will your heart be also.*" (Luke 12:32-34)

"Not because I desire a gift: but I desire fruit that may abound to your account." (Phil. 4:17)

As you give freely to others God will give freely to you.

"But my God shall supply all your need according to his riches in glory by Christ Jesus." (Phil. 4:19)

How Do We Keep Our Prosperity?

If you find you cannot prosper, does it mean that you are in sin? Have you failed to do what God has asked of you? The Scriptures have a great deal to say about this:

> "Thus saith God, *Why transgress ye the command-ments of the LORD, that ye cannot prosper?* because ye have forsaken the LORD, he hath also forsaken you" (2 Chron. 24:20).

> "He that covereth his sins *shall not prosper*: but who-so confesseth and forsaketh them shall have mercy" (Prov. 28:13).

Make sure that the Lord's Prayer is part of your daily time with the Lord. Ask for forgiveness and for the grace you need to forgive others. (See Matt. 6:9-14.)

In summary, how do we obtain prosperity? We obtain prosperity by:

1 Meditating upon and studying the Bible. Make sure you are doing everything it says.
2 Seeking and communing with God.
3 Being rich towards God in tithes and offerings, in every good work, and always remembering the poor.
4 Getting wisdom.
5 Being humble and fearing God.
6 Praying for the peace of Jerusalem. (This is dear to God's heart.)

7   Using your finances for good and not letting them rust.

8   Remembering that the keys to prosperity were given to the patriarchs:

Noah	Righteousness
Abraham	Obedience
Isaac	Inheritance
Jacob	Hard work
Joseph	Sacrifice and suffering

Chapter 7

Tithes, Offerings, and Firstfruits
Giving to God

Tithing

In the beginning of Genesis we can see in the account of Cain and Abel that what differentiates one man from another is often their attitudes regarding giving to God.

How easy it is as a Christian to want to receive from God. We pray, "Forgive me, heal *me*, bless ME, etc. . . . ." But where are those who love to give to God?

The Wise Men brought gold, frankincense, and myrrh to Jesus. The things we can give God are gold (our money), frankincense (living a consecrated life), and myrrh (our willingness to suffer on His behalf).

One way we can give God our money is through tithes. A tithe literally means, a tenth of all income we receive in any way.

The first mention of this word in the Bible occurs when Abraham gives a tithe after his battle in Genesis 14:

> "Then Melchizedek king of Salem brought out bread and wine; he was the priest of God Most High. And he blessed him and said: "Blessed be Abram of God Most High, Possessor of heaven and earth; And blessed be God Most High, Who has delivered your enemies into your hand." And *he gave him a tithe of all"* (Gen. 14:18 NKJV).

Abram, before God changed his name to Abraham, gave a tithe of all that he won in the battle with the Kings. He gave it to the priest of God, Melchizedek, who in turn blessed him and ministered the bread and the wine to him.

Sound familiar?

Jesus is also a Priest after the order of Melchizedek. In the church I attend we always give our tithes and offerings simultaneously as we receive the bread and the wine during communion.

> "So also Christ glorified not himself to be made an high priest; but he that said unto him, Thou art my Son, to day have I begotten thee. As he saith also in another place, Thou art a priest for ever after the order of Melchisedec." (Heb. 5:4-6)

Jacob also promised to give a tenth of all he received to God.

> "And Jacob vowed a vow, saying, If God will be with me, and will keep me in this way that I go, and will give me bread to eat, and raiment to put on, So that I come again to my father's house in peace; then shall the LORD be my God: And this stone, which I have set for a pillar, shall be God's house: *and of all that thou shalt give me I will surely give the tenth unto thee.*" (Gen. 28:20)

Next, we see God setting up tithing in the Law through Moses:

> "And *all the tithe* of the land, whether of the seed of the land or of the fruit of the tree, *is the Lord's*. It is holy to the LORD. 'If a man wants at all to redeem any of his tithes, he shall add one-fifth to it. And concerning the tithe of the herd or the flock, of whatever passes under the rod, *the tenth one* shall be holy to the LORD." (Lev. 27:30 NKJV)

From this we can see that the Israelites were required to give a tenth of the fruit from their lands, their herds, or their flocks. In fact, the Pharisees took this as far as tithing the herbs that grew in their gardens, and Jesus agreed that they should!

> "Woe unto you, scribes and Pharisees, hypocrites! for ye pay tithe of mint and anise and cummin, and have omitted the weightier matters of the law, judgment, mercy, and faith: *these ought ye to have done*, and not to leave the other undone." (Matt. 23:23)

In our modern times, the fruit of our labor is more conventionally paid to us through our wages. Though we must remember not only to give to God what we have earned, but also whatever comes from other means, gifts, dividends, finding something, etc.—any and all income.

God finds many different ways to bless us, and we should be grateful to Him for each of these things in our tithes.

When I was a student, my pastor told me that because I only had a little money I should not tithe out of my grant. I was quite affronted by this, as I had believed his teaching that you prosper as you give. I wondered, "Does he not want me to prosper?!" (Remember the poor widow.)

In spite of what he said to me, I continued tithing, and in approximately my first year of tithing I earned £3,500.

In my second year of tithing I earned £2,500.

In my third year of tithing on a single day I earned approximately £100,000! It is impossible to out-give our God. But what is the purpose of bringing the tithe to church?

> "Behold, I have given the children of Levi all the tithes in Israel as an *inheritance in return for the work which they perform*, the work of the tabernacle of meeting." (Num. 18:21 NKJV)

> "... for the Levites should receive the tithes.... For the children of Israel and the children of Levi shall bring the offering of the grain, of the new wine and the oil, to the storerooms where the articles of the sanctuary are, *where the priests who minister and the gatekeepers and the singers are; and we will not neglect the house of our God.*" (Neh. 10:37 NKJV)

The tithes are for those who work in the house of God—the ministers, the doorkeepers, and the musicians—all who minister the Gospel of Jesus Christ. As God said through Paul and Moses:

> "For it is written in the law of Moses, 'You shall not muzzle an ox while it treads out the grain.' Is it oxen God is concerned about? Or does He say it altogether for our sakes? For our sakes, no doubt, this is written, that he who plows should plow in hope, and he who threshes in hope should be partaker of his hope. If we have sown spiritual things for you, is it a great thing if we reap your material things?" (1 Cor. 9:9 NKJV)

What happens when we don't bring our tithes to church?

> "I also realized that the portions for the Levites had
> not been given them; for *each of the Levites and the
> singers who did the work had gone back to his field*.
> So I contended with the rulers, and said, *'Why is the
> house of God forsaken?'*" (Neh. 13:10 NKJV)

When we don't bring the tithe into the church, then something
has to give, and that normally means that the leaders and musicians who should be laboring in word and prayers have to go and
work in the secular environment to provide for their households.

We all lose out! We need our leaders to be in the Word and in
prayer—on their knees as often as possible.

Another way of looking at it is to remember that we don't own
the tithe anyway.

Who does the tithe belong to? The Bible gives us clear answers
to this question:

> "And all the tithe of the land, whether of the seed of
> the land or of the fruit of the tree, *is the Lord's*. It is
> holy to the LORD" (Lev. 27:30 NKJV).

I particularly like the New International Version translation here:

> "A tithe of everything from the land, whether grain
> from the soil or fruit from the trees, *belongs to the
> LORD*; it is holy to the LORD" (Lev. 27:30 NIV).

We see here that the Bible says that the tithe belongs to the Lord: it is His, not ours! It is not ours to give, but it is for us to return it to Him.

When we don't return what does not belong to us, we are involved in stealing. Does that seem like a strong thing for me to say? Let's look in the Book of Malachi to get our answer:

> "Will a man rob God? Yet you have robbed Me! But you say, 'In what way have we robbed You?' In tithes and offerings." (Mal. 3:8 NKJV)

Very simply, this means: One for God, nine for me. One for God, nine for me. One for God, nine for me. One for God, nine for me. One for God, nine for me. One for God, nine for me. One for God, nine for me.

Not such a bad deal, really.

There are some who would suggest that we don't have to tithe, because tithing is part of the Law.

Well, yes. Tithing is part of the Law, as are not committing adultery, loving God, and honoring your mother and father.

As we have already seen, tithing was here on the Earth before the Law came into being. In fact, tithing was revealed to us in the same breath as the Melchizedek priesthood was revealed to us. This priesthood, which ministered the bread and the wine and received tithes, is the same priesthood that is now in existence. In fact, the only commandment we know about this priesthood is that they should receive tithes!!!

Jesus is the High Priest of the Melchizedek priesthood. (See Heb. 6-7.)

In our lives we learn to turn our life into money through our work. We exchange our time—a portion of our life—into money.

It seems right that as Abram received the bread and the wine, representing Jesus' life, that Abram should also give the tithes, representing his life.

As Jesus has given us his life, his flesh and blood, it is only right that we should give him our life, money earned throughout time (life).

As a businessman, I would say this seems to be a good contract.

Offerings

Now that we have looked at tithing, what other types of offerings does the Bible discuss?

As we study the Law of Moses, we see that there were many kinds of offerings. How do these offerings affect us now, in the New Covenant?

Atonement Money, Burnt Offerings, Drink Offering, Free Offerings, Freewill Offerings, Heave Offering, Meat Offering, Grain Offering, Offer Praise, Offer Sacrifices of Joy, Offer Sacrifices of Righteousness, Offer Unto God Thanksgivings, Offer Up Spiritual Sacrifices, Offered Incense, Offered Themselves, Offering Made by Fire, Offering of Jealousy, Offering of memorial, Passover Offerings, Peace Offerings, Sacrifice of Thanksgiving, Sin/Trespass Offering, Thank Offerings, The First of Thy Ripe

Fruits- Liquors and Firstborn, Voluntary Offerings, Vows, Wave Offering, Wood Offering.

In looking at the offerings that have been given to God from the beginning of time, we can see that many of them are no longer relevant because of Jesus' sacrifice as the Lamb of God. Therefore, there is no more offering for sin.

For me, the most appropriate way to categorize them is: 1) atoning positional offerings, and 2) relational offerings.

Examples of Atoning Offerings

Sin/Trespass Offerings. These are no longer relevant because Jesus' blood redeems us.

> *"Sacrifice and offering and burnt offerings and offering for sin thou wouldest not, neither hadst pleasure therein; which are offered by the law*; …We are sanctified through the offering of the body of Jesus Christ once for all…. *But this man, after he had offered one sacrifice for sins for ever, sat down on the right hand of God*; … *Now where remission of these is, there is no more offering for sin.*" (Heb. 10:5-18)

The burnt offering (Hebrew עֹלָה - *olah*) involves the whole animal being burnt.

The drink offering—this involves wine usually presented with a burnt offering.

Wave and Heave offerings were particular parts of the offerings that were either waved or heaved (lifted up and down) to the

Lord. These parts, the breast and the shoulder, were eaten by the priests and their families.

Examples of Relational Offerings

Free-will Offerings—this type of offering, as the name suggests, is one that comes from a person's free will. An example of this is seen when Moses collected gold, silver, brass, and precious stones for the work of building the Tabernacle in the wilderness. (See Exod. 35.)

In this type of offering, nobody was compelled to bring anything; it was for those with willing hearts—those who want to give to God. This is a quite common type of offering for those of us in the New Testament in cases where money is raised for a good work or project. For example, in the church I attend, we regularly give an offering to help the poor who are living on the streets of London.

Vows—A vow is a promise we make to God. Usually it follows this format: IF you do this, I WILL do that.

Examples of Vows

Jacob promised to give God a tenth of his income if God would bless him.

Hannah promised that if God gave her a son, she would give the child to Him.

Jephthah promised that if God would give him victory over Ammon, then he would offer as a burnt offering "whatsoever comes out of the doors of his house."(This turned out to be his daughter!)

A Note of Warning

One day I was boasting to a friend about God's ability to do anything. When I said that "God could give to me a pair of Prestige clarinets within a day, and that when he would do so, I would ring her to let her know." I said this so that she would see the power of God. Bear in mind that I was a student with no financial means of my own and that these clarinets cost approximately £5,000.00!

Within the same day my agent rang me to say that the company who manufactured these clarinets would sponsor me by giving them to me. I was very pleased, but I forgot to tell my friend!

For various reasons I did not receive those clarinets after all! A couple of years later I was again offered these clarinets and again it did not happen. After the third attempt failed, I was talking to God about it saying how strange it was that every time I tried to get these clarinets something went wrong, when he reminded me of my vow that I would ring my friend when God first came through! As I remembered my mistake I inwardly blushed. I had made a promise to God and broken it.

> "When you make a vow to God, do not delay to pay it; For He has no pleasure in fools. Pay what you have vowed—Better not to vow than to vow and not pay." (Eccles. 5:4 NKJV)

After praying and repenting of my sin, I received the new clarinets very quickly!
You see, not paying my vow caused a blockage in my life. When I repented, the blockage was removed.

What is it that moves us to bring offerings to God?

Offerings are made to God in Genesis before the Law, according to the Law of Moses and in the New Testament, as well.

What Are Offerings For?
Do We Give Offerings Now?

The Law is really quite simple to follow: do this, do that, then do the next thing. But how did Abel and Cain know about giving offerings to God? The truth is we don't know how they knew. There is no account of them learning it from their parents, Adam and Eve, yet "In the process of time they brought an offering." Either they learned it from their parents, or they learned it directly from God, or it was already stored in their souls in the same way that birds know when to fly south and where to go.

Why did they give to God? Surely God doesn't need anything? Do their offerings involve created beings helping out the Creator a bit? I don't think so, yet we are given the opportunity to give to Him, which is a marvelous privilege indeed.

We see from the account of Abel and Cain, that when Abel had given his offering to God, the Lord had respect for Abel and his offering. On the other hand, when Cain brought his offering, he and his offering *were not* respected.

> "Now Abel was a keeper of sheep, but Cain was a tiller of the ground. And in the process of time it came to pass that Cain brought an offering of the fruit of the ground to the LORD. Abel also brought of the firstborn of his flock *and of their fat*. And the LORD respected Abel and his offering, but He did not respect Cain and his offering. And Cain was very angry, and his countenance fell. So the LORD said to Cain,

"Why are you angry? And why has your countenance fallen? If you do well, will you not be accepted? And if you do not do well, sin lies at the door. And its desire *is* for you, but you should rule over it." (Gen. 4:2-7 NKJV)

If you do well, will you not be accepted?

Where Do You Belong?

With maturity comes responsibility. In any group, whether it's a family, a nation, or a kingdom, there is a responsibility to make a contribution to the general upkeep. In a family we share the bills, in a nation we pay our taxes, and in a kingdom we show our allegiance by our support.

Abel did not just bring his contribution; he carefully chose the best, the fattest. He and his offering were respected. Though most of the Kingdom of Heaven was situated in the stars above, his commitment to God and God's kingdom was shown through the quality of his contribution.

Exactly what was wrong with Cain's offering we are not sure. Suffice to say that the Lord did not respect his contribution and in turn he was not respected or accepted. Though not accepted, Cain was not rejected. "If you do well, will you not be accepted?" The alternative to not being accepted in God's society is to be a member of the other community. "If you do not do well, sin lies at the door. And its desire is for you, but you should rule over it."

Note here how sin is personified: "Its desire is for you." Make no mistake about it: sin wants you. It wants to own you. Remember the Scripture that tells us that when we sin, we become a slave to the sin. (See John 8:34.)

God does not need our money, *but*, by giving us the opportunity to give to Him, He is in fact honoring us by giving us the room to be contributors. We are citizens and we become shareholders in the Kingdom of God!

If we hold back and are selfish, then we are not deemed *accepted*?! Where is our allegiance?

The first recorded thing that Noah did after coming out of the ark was to offer burnt offerings of every clean animal and bird to the LORD.

In a burnt offering the animal is completely burnt up; nothing is left—just ashes. Through this means it was thought that the animal was being offered up completely to God. Does this mean that the spirit of the animal went to be with God in Heaven? Having not been to Heaven, it is difficult for anyone to confirm this. Solomon said,

> "Who knows if the spirit of man rises upward and if
> the spirit of the animal goes down into the earth?"
> (Eccles. 3:21 NIV)

Who knows?

Well, God knows.
Whatever happens to the spirit of the animal when it is burnt is, of course, completely within God's control, for that animal has passed over to Him.

So why did Noah offer these animals to God? We know from Genesis 7 that Noah entered the ark with two of every unclean animal and seven of every clean animal. So why did he think he could spare one of every clean animal to be given over to God?

From Genesis 7:11 and Genesis 8:13-14, we can see that Noah was in the ark for slightly over one year! What an experience that must have been. How many people do you suppose were on the Earth before the flood? We know that there were enough people to fill the earth with violence. (See Gen. 6:11.)

It is difficult to know whether that means there were more people alive then than now or less.

But to fill the Earth with anything would require a lot of people.

Imagine the thoughts of Noah while he was in the ark. Apart from the seven people, seven of each of the clean animals, and two of each of the unclean animals that were within the ark, every other person and animal drowned. Was it billions of people? It might well have been.

"Why was I saved—why me?" must have been a question that was in the minds of those on board the ark.

He has one year to contemplate the enormity of the situation. But remember, he did attempt to find out, by sending forth the birds, when the end of his confinement would take place. He did not know that it would only be one year! Like everyone who experiences prolonged confinement, I'm sure he must have been thinking, "What is the first thing I am going to do when I am released?"

The first recorded thing Noah did was to build an altar and offer as burnt offerings one of every clean animal.

It was a mixture of gratitude and the fear of the Lord.

Let us consider how God reacted to the offering. First of all, He was not happy with mankind.

> "And GOD saw that the wickedness of man was great in the earth, and that every imagination of the thoughts of his heart was only evil continually. And it repented the LORD that he had made man *on the earth*, and it grieved him at his heart. And the LORD said, I will destroy man whom I have created from the face of the earth; both man, and beast, and the creeping things, and the fowls of the air; for it repenteth me that I have made them." (Gen. 6:5)

We know from the Scriptures that God is very longsuffering. He is always ready to forgive, and He is full of mercy. At this point He must have been very fed up. He knew what was happening on the Earth: evil, violence, evil thoughts, and wickedness.

God had been putting up with man's evil thoughts for a long time. Even after the plan for the ark was put into operation, there were years waiting for the completion of the construction of the ark. During this time the Earth was full of evil.

When you create millions and billions of souls and they are continually evil, except for one man, it must be extremely disappointing. It truly grieved God in His heart. He also said that he repented of making mankind. At first the idea that God repented of making us is quite shocking. But I think this is explained in Genesis 6:6 where He says that He repents of making us on the

Earth. Perhaps he had considered making us in Heaven rather
than on the Earth? I don't think we can imagine the burden and
grief that God had to endure during this time. Even after the destruction of so many souls, we know that there was a period of
just over a year before life returned to the Earth through the ark.
We should consider what was happening in the Spirit realm during this time. It must have been quite some administration and
processing feat to cope with so many souls passing over all at
the same time. Remember, it took six days to create this world,
but this was a period of just over a year!!

So in response to all of this, Noah offers up one of each of the
clean animals as a burnt offering.

> "And Noah builded an altar unto the LORD; and took
> of every clean beast, and of every clean fowl, and
> offered burnt offerings on the altar. And the LORD
> smelled a sweet savour; and the LORD said in his
> heart, I will not again curse the ground any more for
> man's sake; for the imagination of man's heart is evil
> from his youth; neither will I again smite any more
> every thing living, as I have done. While the earth
> remaineth, seedtime and harvest, and cold and heat,
> and summer and winter, and day and night shall not
> cease. And God blessed Noah and his sons, and said
> unto them, Be fruitful, and multiply, and replenish the
> earth." (Gen. 8:20)

And the LORD smelled a sweet savour. What do you think God
could smell? Was it burning meat? God could smell something
pleasant from the Earth. That smell was a man doing something
that was not evil, doing something that was not self-motivated.
It was the sweet aroma of a man trying to give something back
to Him! Well, that changes the whole picture.

God describes the sensation He receives when we give something to Him as being of a sweet-smelling savour. What smells pleasant to most of us? Perhaps a rose, perfume, incense? When we're hungry, the aroma of a good meal smells good.

> "God immediately responds to this offering by saying, "I will not again curse the ground any more for man's sake: "And God blessed Noah and his sons, and said unto them, Be fruitful, and multiply, and replenish the earth." (Gen. 9:1)

The next mention of offerings is one of the big tests of mankind. Would a man love and trust God enough to offer up "his only begotten son."

The man to whom this test came was Abraham. As we know, he passed the test with flying colors because he was willing to offer up his only begotten son to God.

> "Then the Angel of the LORD called to Abraham a second time out of heaven, and said: "By Myself I have sworn, says the LORD, because you have done this thing, and have not withheld your son, your only son -blessing I will bless you, and multiplying I will multiply your descendants as the stars of the heaven and as the sand which *is* on the seashore; and your descendants shall possess the gate of their enemies. "In your seed all the nations of the earth shall be blessed, because you have obeyed My voice." (Gen. 22:15-18 NKJV)

On request we see Abraham offering up such a precious gift to God. But God's response, as in the case of Noah, was to bless the giver.

"So Israel took his journey with all that he had, and came to Beersheba, and offered sacrifices to the God of his father Isaac. Then God spoke to Israel in the visions of the night, and said, 'Jacob, Jacob!' And he said, 'Here I am.' So He said, 'I am God, the God of your father; do not fear to go down to Egypt, for I will make of you a great nation there. I will go down with you to Egypt, and I will also surely bring you up again; and Joseph will put his hand on your eyes." (Gen. 46:1-4 NKJV)

Again, we see with Israel that after he had sacrificed, *then* God spoke to him.

When we offer something to God, God responds to us. This is a very important precept. If you need a response from God then give Him an offering. You will get His attention, that you are serious.

Firstfruits

The first mention of firstfruits in the Bible is found in Exodus 23, when God asks Moses to set up three feasts in the year. It is the second of these feasts—"The feast of Harvest," in which the children of Israel were required to bring in the firstfruits from their labors in the field.

After the firstfruits of the harvest were collected, they were given to Aaron and to his descendants, the priests who minister in the house of God. They presented a small portion of the offering, a memorial, to God with the remainder to be eaten by them and their families.

From Nehemiah we can see that the ministers who received the firstfruits also included the gatekeepers and singers.

> "I also realized that the portions for the Levites had not been given them; for each of the Levites and the singers who did the work had gone back to his field. So I contended with the rulers, and said, "Why is the house of God forsaken?" (Neh. 13:10-11 NKJV)

When we neglect the house of God, those who are chosen to do the work have to find secular work to fulfil their needs!

Are the churches filled with choirs and orchestras, or do the musicians work in the world for their living and do part-time work for the churches? Is your pastor fully supported by the church, or does he have other part-time or full-time work to do to support himself and his family?

When you get a new job or start a new business venture, consider how to apportion the firstfruits unto the Lord.

Being grateful to God in this way pleases Him and helps support His Church.

Chapter 8

Sowing and Reaping

It is important for us to understand the concept of sowing and reaping. For the Christian it is a fundamental law of prosperity and also a fact of life for everyone on this Earth.

God could have chosen to give us a life in which we did not have to grow. He could have provided all the money, food, drink, clothes, necessities, and luxuries in great quantities for each soul—unlimited provisions for everybody.

One could say that the Garden of Eden was almost like that; yet even there Adam had to tend and keep the Garden. (See Gen. 2:15.)

God has chosen, however, to give each of us a life that is dependent on sowing and reaping. If you work for someone, then you sow your time and labor and you reap your wages. In business you sow, advertise, and reap; then you close the sale. In evangelism we sow the Word, and we reap when the soul becomes a Christian and grows into a disciple.

Jesus sowed His own life in order to reap our lives!

> "Verily, verily, I say unto you, Except a corn of wheat fall into the ground and die, it abideth alone: but if it die, it bringeth forth much fruit." (John 12:24)

Cain and Abel were born to Adam and Eve. Both their jobs involved sowing and reaping.

> "And Adam knew Eve his wife; and she conceived, and bare Cain, and said, I have gotten a man from the LORD. And she again bare his brother Abel. And Abel was a keeper of sheep, but Cain was a tiller of the ground." (Gen. 4:1)

Abel was a shepherd and Cain was a tiller of the ground. Both of their jobs involved sowing and reaping. Cain would sow the seed into the ground and at the time of harvest he would reap the grain.

Abel would tend the sheep, and the rams would impregnate the ewes with their seed. The time of reaping would take place when the lambs would give birth.

In Matthew chapter 13 we have a portion of Scripture that describes the purpose, beginning, and end of this world in terms of sowing and reaping.

The kingdom of heaven is likened unto a man which sowed good seed in his field: But while men slept, his enemy came and sowed tares among the wheat, and went his way. (Read Matt.13:24-43 in the KJV.)

God is sowing His children, and His enemy, Satan, is sowing his children, but the outcome is good for God's children!

Sowing and reaping are facts of life for everyone on this Earth. It is the law of cause and effect—what you sow you will reap. This has been recognized in other religions, as well; in fact, the Buddhist and Hindu religions refer to it as *Karma*.

Sowing and Reaping Scriptures

If you sow wickedness, you will reap wickedness.

> "Even as I have seen, they that plow iniquity, and sow wickedness, reap the same." (Job 4:8)

If you sow tears, you will reap joy.

> "They that sow in tears shall reap in joy. He that goeth forth and weepeth, bearing precious seed, shall doubtless come again with rejoicing, bringing his sheaves with him." (Ps. 126:5)

If you sow righteousness, you will reap your reward.

> "The wicked worketh a deceitful work: but to him that soweth righteousness shall be a sure reward." (Prov. 11:18)

If you sow righteousness, you will reap mercy. If you sow wickedness, you will reap iniquity.

> "Sow to yourselves in righteousness, reap in mercy; break up your fallow ground: for it is time to seek the LORD, till he come and rain righteousness upon you. Ye have plowed wickedness, ye have reaped iniquity." (Hos. 10:12)

If you sow to your flesh, you will reap corruption. If you sow to the Spirit, you shall reap everlasting life.

> "For he that soweth to his flesh shall of the flesh reap corruption; but he that soweth to the Spirit shall of the Spirit reap life everlasting." (Gal. 6:8)

We can sum it up with the following Scripture, which tells us that what you give, you will get back in even greater measure. This is true for good or evil and for Christian or non-Christian alike.

> "Give, and it will be given to you: good measure, pressed down, shaken together, and running over will be put into your bosom. For with the same measure that you use, it will be measured back to you." (Luke 6:38 NKJV)

When we reap, we should remember the poor and our ministers. Do not be misled into believing that all you reap belongs to you.

> "And when ye reap the harvest of your land, thou shalt not wholly reap the corners of thy field, neither shalt thou gather the gleanings of thy harvest. And thou shalt not glean thy vineyard, neither shalt thou gather every grape of thy vineyard; thou shalt *leave them for the poor and stranger*: I am the LORD your God." (Lev. 19:9-10)

> "Speak unto the children of Israel, and say unto them, When ye be come into the land which I give unto you, and shall reap the harvest thereof, then ye shall bring a sheaf of the firstfruits of your harvest *unto the priest*." (Lev. 23:10)

> "*Let him that is taught in the word communicate unto him that teacheth in all good things.* Be not deceived; God is not mocked: for whatsoever a man soweth, that shall he also reap. For he that soweth to his flesh shall of the flesh reap corruption; but he that soweth to the Spirit shall of the Spirit reap life everlasting." (Gal. 6:6-8)

Sometimes one can sow, but before it becomes time to reap the seed does not grow or it all gets destroyed. Why is that?

Satan will try and devour what you should be reaping. Make sure that you are giving your tithes and offerings so that the Lord can rebuke the devourer for your sake. Also make sure that you are building God's kingdom through your work and through the church. Always check your motives.

> "Will a man rob God? Yet ye have robbed me. But ye say, Wherein have we robbed thee? In tithes and offerings. *Ye are cursed with a curse: for ye have robbed me*, even this whole nation. *Bring ye all the tithes into the storehouse*, that there may be meat in mine house, and prove me now herewith, saith the LORD of hosts, if I will not open you the windows of heaven, and pour you out a blessing, that there shall not be room enough to receive it. *And I will rebuke the devourer for your sakes*, and he shall not destroy the fruits of your ground; neither shall your vine cast her fruit before the time in the field, saith the LORD of hosts." (Mal. 3:8-12)

> "Now therefore thus saith the LORD of hosts; Consider your ways. Ye have sown much, and bring in little; ye eat, but ye have not enough; ye drink, but ye are not filled with drink; ye clothe you, but there is none warm; and he that earneth wages earneth wages to put it into a bag with holes. Thus saith the LORD of hosts; *Consider your ways. Go up to the mountain, and bring wood, and build the house; and I will take pleasure in it, and I will be glorified, saith the LORD.*" (Hag. 1:5-8)

In sowing and reaping let us not forget the effect of rain. Without rain no seed will grow. The rain comes from Heaven. If God withholds it, a nation will have famine; if He gives it, then the seed will grow. God uses famine as one of His judgments.

> "For thus saith the Lord GOD; How much more when I send my four sore judgments upon Jerusalem, the sword, and the famine, and the noisome beast, and the pestilence, to cut off from it man and beast?" (Ezek. 14:21)

If you need to prosper, my advice to you is to get on with it. Start sowing, give to good causes, and make sure you are tithing and giving offerings. Look around your home to see if there is something you are not using and give it to someone in need. Many blockages to finances can be unblocked through giving. Don't let your life stagnate.

Solomon tells us to stop looking at the wind, to get on with it. You don't need to understand how it works. Just know that it does.

> "*He that observeth the wind shall not sow*; and he that regardeth the clouds shall not reap." (Eccles. 11:4)

Finally, let us not forget Paul's admonition, which declares that you will reap according to how you sow:

> "But this I say, He which soweth sparingly shall reap also sparingly; and he which soweth bountifully shall reap also bountifully. Every man according as he purposeth in his heart, so let him give; not grudgingly, or of necessity: for *God loveth a cheerful giver*. And God is able to make all grace abound toward you; that

ye, always having all sufficiency in all things, may abound to every good work." (2 Cor. 9:6)

Chapter 9

Entering the Promised Land

"How long will you neglect to go and possess the land which the LORD God of your fathers has given you?" (Josh. 18:3 NKJV)

On leaving Egypt the children of Israel were given a promise that the LORD would bring them into the Promised Land. It was to be a land flowing with milk and honey.

We have been given similar promises, though not an actual land—yet. We, those who belong to Christ, have been promised the inheritance of the blessings that were given to Abraham. (See Gal. 3:29.)

By observing how Israel was able to obtain the Promised Land, we can see a mirrored portrayal of how we should obtain our promises.

"I have surely seen the oppression of My people who are in Egypt"... *"So I have come down to deliver them out of the hand of the Egyptians, and to bring them up from that land to a good and large land, to a land flowing with milk and honey,* ... "Come now, therefore, and I will send you to Pharaoh that you may

bring My people, the children of Israel, out of Egypt."
(Exod. 3:7-8 NKJV)

After the children of Israel had come out of Egypt, Moses sent
twelve spies, one from each tribe of Israel, to spy out the Promised Land. This is the account of their experience:

> "Then Moses sent them to spy out the land of Ca-
> naan... "We went to the land where you sent us. *It
> truly flows with milk and honey, and this is its fruit....*
> Then Caleb quieted the people before Moses, and said,
> *"Let us go up at once and take possession, for we are
> well able to overcome it."* But the men who had gone
> up with him said, *"We are not able to go up against
> the people, for they are stronger than we."* And they
> gave the children of Israel a bad report of the land
> which they had spied out....And *all the children of
> Israel complained against Moses and Aaron...* (See
> Num. 13:16-15:1 NKJV)

After all the miracles that the LORD did in bringing them out
of Egypt, most of Israel failed to get into the Promised Land
because of unbelief.

Prerequisites for Obtaining God's Promises

The first prerequisite for obtaining promises from God is that
you *must* have *faith*.

> "Take heed, brethren, lest there be in any of you
> *an evil heart of unbelief,* in departing from the liv-
> ing God. But exhort one another daily, while it is
> called To day; lest any of you be hardened through
> the deceitfulness of sin. For we are made partakers

of Christ, if we hold the beginning of our confidence stedfast unto the end; While it is said, To day if ye will hear his voice, harden not your hearts, as in the provocation. For some, when they had heard, did provoke: howbeit not all that came out of Egypt by Moses. But with whom was he grieved forty years? *was it* not with them that had sinned, whose carcases fell in the wilderness? And to whom sware he that they should not enter into his rest, but to them that believed not? So we see *that they could not enter in because of unbelief.*" (Heb. 3:12-5:1)

It was left for Joshua to lead the children into the Promised Land. In the first chapter of Joshua we see the second prerequisite for obtaining promises from God:

"Moses My servant is dead. Now therefore, arise, go over this Jordan, you and all this people, to the land which I am giving to them....Only be strong and very courageous, *that you may observe to do* according to all the law which Moses My servant commanded you; do not turn from it to the right hand or to the left, *that you may prosper wherever you go.* This Book of the Law shall not depart from your mouth, but you shall meditate in it day and night, that you may observe to do according to all that is written in it. For then *you will make your way prosperous*, and then you will have good success. Have I not commanded you? Be strong and of good courage; do not be afraid, nor be dismayed, for the LORD your God is with you wherever you go. " (Josh. 1:1-11 NKJV)

Know the Word of God

The second prerequisite is that you must know the Word of God; you must study it and then most important, you must obey it. Success comes from obeying God and knowing His promises.

The Promised Land is a land flowing with milk and honey. This is a beautiful picture, but the Scriptures about the Promised Land are there for more than just art, poetry, beauty, and hope.

When Joshua and the Israelites went into the Promised Land, they were not invited in by the inhabitants of that land. In fact, they had to take the land by force.

Without the action of a force upon us, our lives will stay the same. If you want to obtain a promise of God, you have to apply a force. Life does not just change itself. Sometimes you have to fight in order to obtain your "promised land."

And from the days of John the Baptist until now the kingdom of heaven suffereth violence, and the violent take it by force. (Matt. 11:12)

> *"Fight the good fight* of faith, *lay hold on eternal life*, to which you were also called and have confessed the good confession in the presence of many witnesses." (1Tim. 6:12 NKJV)

We need to lay hold on eternal life, and we need to lay hold of the Promised Land.

When Joshua entered the Promised Land, he had to fight. If you want to enter your promised land, you will have to fight, as well. You must remember that your enemy does not want you to prosper. Every penny more that you have is a penny less in his kingdom. We have a saying in England that if you look after the pennies, the pounds will look after themselves.

Satan does not want a shift of economic power into the Kingdom of God, and he will fight you all the way. But we are blessed in that the victory is surely ours; Jesus has been slain so that the blessings would be ours. We need to rise up and take hold of the promises of God. We need to believe them, receive them, and enjoy them.

Faith and Prayer

The third prerequisite for obtaining the promises of God involves applying force by fighting with faith and prayer.

The first battle for the Promised Land was to be against Jericho. Let's take a look at how it was won. Read Joshua chapter 6.

> "And the LORD said to Joshua: "See! I have given Jericho into your hand, its king, and the mighty men of valor. *"You shall march around the city, all you men of war; you shall go all around the city once. This you shall do six days.* "And seven priests shall *bear seven trumpets of rams' horns before the ark. But the seventh day you shall march around the city seven times, and the priests shall blow the trumpets. "It shall come to pass, when they make a long blast with the ram's horn, and when you hear the sound of the trumpet, that all the people shall shout with a great shout; then the wall of the city will fall down flat. And the people shall go up every man straight before him. "*… So the people shouted when the priests

blew the trumpets. And it happened when the people heard the sound of the trumpet, and the people shouted with a great shout, that the wall fell down flat. Then the people went up into the city, every man straight before him, and they took the city. And they utterly destroyed all that was in the city...." (Josh. 6:2-21 NKJV)

Can you imagine the generals who led the troops during the Second World War, Generals Montgomery and Patton, in particular, sitting around a table planning their attacks and saying, "Let's march around the city once for six days and seven times on the seventh day and then blow the trumpets and the walls will fall down."

This is not a normal military strategy. But it does point to an essential strategy for fighting God's battles—*obedience.*

Obedience

The fourth prerequisite for obtaining the promises of God is *obedience.*

The next battle for the children of Israel was a disaster; in fact, it was lost. Why was this? See Joshua chapter 7.

> *"Israel has sinned, and they have also transgressed My covenant which I commanded them.* For they have even taken some of the accursed things, and have both stolen and deceived; and they have also put it among their own stuff. *"Therefore the children of Israel could not stand before their enemies..."* (Josh. 7:11-12)

The children of Israel, because they had sinned, could not stand before their enemies. The perpetrators of the sin had to be burned with fire. They had to be sanctified.

Holiness

The fifth prerequisite for obtaining the promises of God is holiness. When we sin, we are not able to obtain the promises. We have to repent, find out what the blockage may be, and remove it.

The inhabitants of Gibeon avoided destruction through craftiness. Let's see what they did: Read Joshua chapter 9.

Let us remember that our enemy is as crafty as a serpent. He will try and catch us in legal traps. By making a covenant with the Gibeonites the children of Israel had legally allowed snares in Israel which affected them for hundreds of years. (See 2 Sam. 21.)

If they had taken to heart the second prerequisite, which is knowing God's Word, they would not have fallen into the trap.

> *"Take heed to yourself, lest you make a covenant with the inhabitants of the land where you are going, lest it be a snare in your midst."* (Exod. 34:12 NKJV)

Ask for the Lord's Counsel

They could also have avoided the trap by using the sixth prerequisite for obtaining the promises of God: *Ask counsel of the LORD.*

Speaking to Christians, Paul says that we can have filthiness of spirit. It is worth noting that Israel allowed unclean people to dwell in their midst through a legal mechanism. It is important that we do not allow unclean spirits to dwell in our midst through legal rights. This can become a snare to our lives. Release yourself from all spiritual oppression through repentance and the cleansing of the blood of Jesus. (See 1 John 1:7.)

> "Therefore, having these promises, beloved, let us cleanse ourselves from all filthiness of the flesh *and spirit*, perfecting holiness in the fear of God." (2 Cor. 7:1 NKJV)

Perseverance and Patience

The seventh prerequisite for obtaining the promises of God, your Promised Land, is seen in the following verse:

> "Joshua made war *a long time* with all those kings" (Josh. 11:18).

Sometimes things take *a long time*. Therefore, you need to persevere and exercise patience.

> "For God is not unjust to forget your work and labor of love which you have shown toward His name, in that you have ministered to the saints, and do minister. And we desire that each one of you show the same diligence to the full assurance of hope until the end, that you do not become sluggish, but imitate those who *through faith and patience inherit the promises.*" (Heb. 6:10-12 NKJV)

The seventh prerequisite for obtaining the promises of God, therefore, is patience.

Joshua and the children of Israel had seven enemies in the Promised Land. (See Josh. 3:10.)

I like to picture these seven nations as enemies to overcome.

In an individual's personal life I am often able to identify the seven enemies as I have indicated below.

This list consists of my own thoughts, and I am sure you could write your own similar list.

The important thing to remember is that identifying your enemies is the first step towards destroying them.

	Your Enemies	God's Benefits
Canaanites	Sickness	Health
Hittites	Poverty	Prosperity
Hivites	Fear, Anxiety, War	Peace/Rest
Perizzites	Unbelief	Faith
Girgashites	Sin	Forgiveness
Amorites	Disobedience	Obedience
Jebusites	Uncleanness	Holiness

Please remember that the first prerequisite for obtaining promises from God is that you *must* have *faith*.

The second prerequisite is that you must know the Word of God. This means that you must study it and then, most important, obey it. Success comes from obeying God and knowing His promises.

The third prerequisite for obtaining the promises of God is "the applying of force" through fighting with faith and prayer.

The fourth prerequisite for obtaining the promises of God is *obedience*.

The fifth prerequisite for obtaining the promises of God is holiness. When we sin, we are not able to obtain the promises. We have to repent, find out what the blockage may be, and remove it.

The sixth prerequisite for obtaining the promises of God is to *Ask counsel of the LORD*.

The seventh prerequisite for obtaining the promises of God is *patience*.

"Now the whole congregation of the children of Israel assembled together at Shiloh, and set up the tabernacle of meeting there. And the land was subdued before them.

But there remained among the children of Israel seven tribes which had not yet received their inheritance. Then Joshua said to the children of Israel: *"How long will you neglect to go and possess the land which the LORD God of your fathers has given you?"* (Josh. 18:1-3 NKJV)

Read more about the promises of God by studying the Scriptures I've listed here:

Romans 4:19-21
2 Corinthians 1:18-20
Ephesians 1:1-14
Hebrews 4:1-16
Hebrews 6:10-20
Hebrews 9:15-16
James 2:5

2 Peter 1:1-14
1 John 2:25

Chapter 10

The Covenants of God

There are a number of different covenants (or promises) in the Bible. The most significant are those that were given to Noah, Abraham, Moses, and the New Covenant, which came through Jesus.

Simply stated, a covenant is a contract or agreement between two parties.

The first covenant we see in the Bible is the covenant that was made between God and Noah, his seed after him, and every living creature. The nature of this covenant was: "Neither shall all flesh be cut off any more by the waters of a flood; neither shall there any more be a flood to destroy the earth." This was a promise that was made by God, and this promise was without conditions. God also decided to give a token to remind us and Him of this covenant.

> "And God said, This is the token of the covenant which I make between me and you and every living creature that is with you, for perpetual generations: I do set my bow in the cloud, and it shall be for a *token* of a *covenant* between me and the earth. And it shall come to pass, when I bring a cloud over the earth, that the bow shall be seen in the cloud: And I will remember my covenant, which is between me and you

and every living creature of all flesh; and the waters shall no more become a flood to destroy all flesh." (Gen. 9:12)

It is interesting to note that the word used for "bow" also means "iris." God is watching it through the iris of His eye.

This covenant set up by God has never been broken!

Covenants and Promises Made to Abraham

These promises that were made to Abraham come from a series of works Abraham was asked to do. At each step the reward Abraham was given becomes greater and greater. Not only were these promises made to him but also to his descendants and his seed, Jesus, from whom we inherited these promises! It is of the utmost importance to understand what our father Abraham received from God, because we are also co-heirs of these precious promises.

As you read these Scriptures, you will see that sometimes Abraham is referred to as Abram. This is because originally he was named Abram, meaning exalted father, and God later changed his name to Abraham, meaning a father of multitudes (nations).

> "Now the LORD had said to Abram: 'Get out of your country, From your family And from your father's house, To a land that I will show you. *I will make you a great nation; I will bless you And make your name great; And you shall be a blessing. I will bless those who bless you, And I will curse him who curses you; And in you all the families of the earth shall be blessed."* So Abram departed as the LORD had spoken to him..." (Gen. 12:1-4 NKJV)

We can see from these Scriptures that God asked Abram to do something: "Get out of your country, from your family and from your father's house, to a land that I will show you." There is a reward for doing what God commands: *I will make you a great nation; I will bless you And make your name great; And you shall be a blessing. I will bless those who bless you, And I will curse him who curses you; And in you all the families of the earth shall be blessed.*

Abram was asked to leave his home, his country, and his family. This was not a small request from God. Abram was not forced to do it; God asked him to. We have to love God more than anything, more than our homes, our country, and our family. Where would we be if Abram had said, "No"? Did God ask anybody else first; did they turn Him down? The reason I say this is because God is always looking for those who will obey Him. Has God asked you to do something? Then do it. If you don't obey God, the Kingdom of Heaven will not fall down. God will simply find somebody who will obey Him, and they will get their reward. Is somebody else at this moment being asked to do the things you have been asked to do?

Abram made a decision to obey God, and he departed as the LORD had directed him to do. The LORD then appeared to Abram and said, "To your descendants I will give this land." Abram had been rewarded for his obedience. God is always faithful to His promises.

> "After these things the word of the LORD came to Abram in a vision, saying, 'Do not be afraid, Abram. I am your shield, your exceedingly great reward.' But Abram said, 'Lord GOD, what will You give me, seeing I go childless…. 'Look now toward heaven, and count the stars if you are able to number them.' And

He said to him, 'So shall your descendants be.' *And
he believed in the LORD*, and He accounted it to him
for righteousness." (Gen. 15:1-6 NKJV)

Here Abram is asked to believe something, *"Look now toward
heaven, and count the stars if you are able to number them."
And He said to him, "So shall your descendants be."*

Let us remember that Abram was over seventy-five years of age
at this time; he was not a young man. God had said to him that
He was his exceedingly great reward. But Abram had something
missing. "What will you give me, seeing I go childless?" Nothing material could cover the hole that Abraham felt in his life. So
how does God respond? "Look now toward heaven, and count
the stars. So shall your descendants be." This must have been a
very hard thing for Abram to believe, considering his age. Yet he
still believed the Lord.

> "Then He brought him outside and said, 'Look now
> toward heaven, and count the stars if you are able to
> number them.' And He said to him, 'So shall your de-
> scendants be.' And he believed in the LORD, and He
> accounted it to him for righteousness." (Gen. 15:5-6
> NKJV)

This one act of faith by Abram was rewarded by God giving
righteousness to him. Do not underestimate the importance of
this event. The whole history of mankind has been shaped by
God giving Abram this righteousness. It is sometimes hard to
understand, yet this righteousness that was given to Abram was a
transferable asset. All of the blessings that were given to Abram
we are able to receive through Jesus and the administration of
Jesus. (See Gal. 3:6-14.)

In the next Scriptures we see God making a covenant with Abram. Abram is asked to walk before God and be blameless. God in turn will multiply his descendants exceedingly, and nations and kings would come from him, and that his name was now to be called Abraham. The sign of this contract was to be circumcision, the cutting away of the foreskin of all males.

> "I am the Almighty God; walk before me, and be thou perfect. And I will make my covenant between me and thee, and will multiply thee exceedingly…. This is my covenant, which ye shall keep, between me and you and thy seed after thee; Every man child among you shall be circumcised… And God said, Sarah thy wife shall bear thee a son indeed; and thou shalt call his name Isaac: and I will establish my covenant with him for an everlasting covenant, and with his seed after him." (Gen. 17:1-7 NKJV)

We can see that not only was this covenant made with Abraham, but it was also to be established in his son of promise, Isaac—a son who would be born to a ninety-year-old woman, Sarah.

Just when things seem hard to believe, they often got harder. But Abraham grew strong in faith; he may have started out laughing, but he obtained the son of promise.

So what was the next test for Abraham? He had already left his family, friends, home, and traveled to a foreign country. He obeyed God, lived blamelessly, walked with God, and *believed* God.

What about giving up the one thing he had lacked, hoped for, and received. How about sacrificing his only begotten son? Does this sound familiar? Read Genesis chapter 22.

> *"God tested Abraham…"*"Take now your son, your
> only son Isaac, whom you love, and go to the land of
> Moriah, and offer him there as a burnt offering…. And
> Abraham stretched out his hand and took the knife
> to slay his son. But the Angel of the LORD called
> to him from heaven and said, "Abraham, Abraham!"
> So he said, "Here I am." And He said, "Do not lay
> your hand on the lad, or do anything to him; for now I
> know that you fear God, since *you have not withheld
> your son, your only son, from Me…* "By Myself I
> have sworn, says the LORD, because you have done
> this thing, and have not withheld your son, your only
> son— "blessing I will bless you, and multiplying
> I will multiply your descendants as the stars of the
> heaven and as the sand which *is* on the seashore; and
> your descendants shall possess the gate of their en-
> emies. "In your seed all the nations of the earth shall
> be blessed, because you have obeyed My voice."
> (Gen. 22:1-18 NKJV)

Abraham did not waste time; he left early in the morning. Imagine what a night that must have been. Did Abraham toss and
turn all night? Something monumental was to happen; a def-
inite deadline was coming up. Three days it took to travel to
the appointed place of sacrifice, and that was plenty of time to
change one's mind. Was it God who spoke, or was it not God
who spoke? We don't know what was going through Abraham's
mind. He believed he was to be the father of nations, yet God
was asking him to sacrifice his son, Isaac. How could he sacrifice the son through whom the promises were to come? The only
answer was that God must be able to raise him from the dead.

This we know Abraham thought, because it says so in Hebrews
11:19:

> "By faith Abraham, when he was tried, offered up
> Isaac: and he that had received the promises offered
> up his only begotten son, Of whom it was said, That
> in Isaac shall thy seed be called: *Accounting that God
> was able to raise him up, even from the dead*; from
> whence also he received him in a figure" (Heb. 11:17-
> 19 NKJV).

This testing of Abraham's faith and obedience, I believe, goes far beyond his own situation.

I believe this was a proving of mankind. Thus, when Jesus said that He was to be raised from the dead on the third day, the faith of Jesus could not be refuted. What I mean is that Satan could not question the validity of the faith employed by the son of man by saying "It is not in mankind to be able to believe that a man could be raised from the dead!" The Father could quite easily say, "Look at my friend Abraham; he believed I could raise Isaac from the dead!"

It was not only Jesus that had faith to rise from the dead.

God was so moved by Abraham's willingness to sacrifice his only begotten son and his willingness to believe that God was able to raise him from the dead that He decided to bless Abraham.

This blessing was special; first of all, God swore an oath. As there is nothing higher than himself, he swore by himself.

> "*By Myself I have sworn*, says the LORD, because
> you have done this thing, and have not withheld your
> son, your only son—"blessing I will bless you, and
> multiplying I will multiply your descendants as the
> stars of the heaven and as the sand which is on the
> seashore; and your descendants shall possess the gate

of their enemies. "In your seed all the nations of the
earth shall be blessed, because you have obeyed My
voice." (Gen. 22:16-18 NKJV)

The Promises

"Blessing I will bless you." This phrase is so small, yet so *huge.*
The ramifications stretch to every believer who has lived after
Abraham. This is because this blessing was passed as an inheritance
through Isaac and Jacob/Israel and to the Gentiles through Jesus.

> "In Christ Jesus the blessing of Abraham might come
> to the Gentiles, so that we would receive the promise
> of the Spirit through faith." (Gal. 3:14 NASB)

If I promise to bless you by saying, "Blessing, I will bless you,"
then I can do so to the limit of everything I possess.

If a king were to bless you by saying, "Blessing, I will bless you,"
then the limit of blessing will be that which the king possesses.

Similarly, when Almighty God says, "Blessing, I will bless you."
What is the limit of this blessing? We can see from the verse of
Galatians quoted above that included in what God possesses is
His Spirit. This is linked to the promise that was given to Abra-
ham as part of the blessings.

When trying to find the limits of the blessings given to Abraham,
I try to imagine what is the most precious thing I know God has?
Of course that has to be His Son, Jesus.

> "He who did not spare His own Son, but delivered
> Him over for us all, how will He not also with Him
> freely give us all things?" (Rom. 8:32 NKJV)

We can see that God has held nothing back in blessings, and He has said that with Him, that is, Jesus, He will freely give us all things.

Did God bless Abraham in all things?

> "And he said, I am Abraham's servant. And the LORD hath blessed my master greatly; and he is become great: and he hath given him flocks, and herds, and silver, and gold, and menservants, and maidservants, and camels, and asses." (Gen. 24:34-35)

> "And Abraham was old, and well stricken in age: and the LORD had blessed Abraham *in all things*." (Gen. 24:1)

The whole universe, the heavens and the Earth, are governed by laws. God's justice decrees that righteousness is observed from the heavenly perspective at all times. Even God limits himself at times by means of His Word, thereby giving us stability.

We see this mirrored in Scripture when King Darius could not undo a law that he made; therefore, he condemned Daniel to the lions' den.

Even though King Darius did not want Daniel to be put into the lions' den, he could not stop it, because he had to enforce the law that he had decreed. (See Dan. 6.)

Even God cannot do what He wants to, when He limits himself by His own Word. This is why the human soul has free will on Earth. This is why we have the freedom to kill and to love; we have the power of choice. Of course, it is not God's will for us to murder, but it is His will for us to love. Why do we pray, "Thy will be done on earth as it is in heaven," if His will is being done?

Has God given himself the freedom to bless anybody whenever He wants to? I don't know, but what I do know is that He has blessed Abraham and his seed, which is Jesus, and through Jesus He has blessed me!

Is this in Scripture, and can I be blessed as well?

> "Christ has redeemed us from the curse of the law, having become a curse for us (for it is written, "Cursed is everyone who hangs on a tree"), *that the blessing of Abraham might come upon the Gentiles in Christ Jesus, that we might receive the promise of the Spirit through faith.* Brethren, I speak in the manner of men: Though it is only a man's covenant, yet if it is confirmed, *no one annuls or adds to it.* Now to Abraham and his Seed were the promises made. He does not say, "And to seeds," as of many, but as of one, "And to your Seed," who is Christ. And this I say, that the law, which was four hundred and thirty years later, *cannot annul the covenant* that was confirmed before by God in Christ, that it should make the promise of no effect. For *if the inheritance is of the law, it is no longer of promise*; but God gave it to Abraham by promise. What purpose then does the law serve? It was added because of transgressions, till the Seed should come to whom the promise was made; and it was appointed through angels by the hand of a mediator. Now a mediator does not mediate for one only, but God is one. Is the law then against the promises of God? Certainly not! For if there had been a law given which could have given life, truly righteousness would have been by the law. But the Scripture has confined all under sin, *that the promise by faith in Jesus Christ might be given to those who believe.*

But before faith came, we were kept under guard by the law, kept for the faith which would afterward be revealed. Therefore the law was our tutor to bring us to Christ, that we might be justified by faith. But after faith has come, we are no longer under a tutor. For you are all sons of God through faith in Christ Jesus. For as many of you as were baptized into Christ have put on Christ." (Gal. 3:13-27)

It seems to me that God has placed a "trust fund" on the Earth for His children. This trust fund was set up by God, through Abraham's works, to be received by Jesus and then inherited by the rest of the children of God.

"Blessed be the God and Father of our Lord Jesus Christ, *who has blessed us with every spiritual blessing in the heavenly places in Christ*... having predestined us to adoption as sons by Jesus Christ to Himself." (Eph. 1:3 NKJV)

And for this reason He is the Mediator of the new covenant, by means of death, for the redemption of the transgressions under the first covenant, that those who are called *may receive the promise of the eternal inheritance.* (Heb. 9:15)

I would also go so far as to say that it is because of this promise to Abraham that we are legally entitled to pray for things. This is why we can pray for them in faith, because they have already been paid for.

"Jesus answered and said unto them, Verily I say unto you, If ye have faith, and doubt not, ye shall not only do this which is done to the fig tree, but also if ye shall say unto this mountain, Be thou removed, and be thou cast into the sea; it shall be done. *And all things, whatsoever ye shall ask in prayer, believing, ye shall receive."* (Matt. 21:20-22)

To receive from the trust fund, all you need is faith and patience. (See Heb. 6:12.)

Chapter 11

The Inheritance

When the Israelites were going into the Promised Land, they were told that it was going to be their inheritance. But they had to fight for it. The land was to be divided up by lot and then passed through to the next generations through the tribes and families.

> "And you shall divide the land by lot as an inheritance among your families; to the larger you shall give a larger inheritance, and to the smaller you shall give a smaller inheritance; there everyone's inheritance shall be whatever falls to him by lot. You shall inherit according to the tribes of your fathers." (Num. 33:54 NKJV)

The land that the Israelites were to inherit was flowing with milk and honey; in fact, it was such a blessing that there was a real possibility of having no poor people there at all!

> "Except when there may be no poor among you; for the LORD will greatly bless you in the land which the LORD your God is giving you to possess as an inheritance." (Deut. 15:4 NKJV)

Now as we know from an earthly point of view, if we are to inherit something, someone has to die. So who died, and what did we inherit?

Let us read the following Scripture carefully:

> "But Christ came as High Priest… with His own blood He entered the Most Holy Place once for all, having obtained eternal redemption… And for this reason *He is the Mediator of the new covenant*, by means of death, *for the redemption of the transgressions under the first co*venant, that those who are called *may receive the promise of the eternal inheritance.* For where there is a testament, there must also of necessity be the death of the testator. For a testament is in force after men are dead, since it has no power at all while the testator lives" (Heb. 9:11-18 NKJV).

Jesus died; He was crucified on the cross. But this was a travesty of justice. The wages of sin is death, yet Jesus had not sinned. Therefore, God intervened and raised Him from the dead.

But the plain fact is that He did die. Therefore, His property, whether physical or spiritual, can be legally passed on as an inheritance. A last will and testament is in force after a person is dead.

It is appointed for a man to die once and then the judgment. (See Heb. 9:27.)

What was Jesus' judgment?

Let's see what He told His disciples after He was raised from the dead:

> "Then the eleven disciples went away into Galilee,
> to the mountain which Jesus had appointed for them.
> When they saw Him, they worshiped Him; but some
> doubted. And Jesus came and spoke to them, saying,
> *"All authority has been given to Me in heaven and on
> earth"* (Matt. 28:16-18 NKJV).

All authority in Heaven and on Earth has been given to Jesus. That's quite a reward. Jesus died and His judgment was given to Him. The Father gave Him all authority in Heaven and on Earth. One day we will all have to stand before the Father for our judgment, as well. Therefore, make sure you receive a reward, not condemnation.

What else did He receive?

> "Saying with a loud voice: "Worthy is the Lamb who
> was slain *to receive power and riches* and wisdom,
> And strength and honor and glory and blessing!"
> (Rev. 5:12 NKJV)

Having been raised from the dead, Jesus is in the unusual position of being the administrator of His own estate, and He is able to choose who He gives His belongings to.

Those who serve the Lord Christ receive their inheritance under the administration of Jesus.

> "Knowing that *from the Lord you will receive the
> reward of the inheritance*; for you serve the Lord
> Christ." (Col. 3:24 NKJV)

Does Scripture really say that I have a part in this inheritance?

"And for this reason He is the Mediator of the new
covenant, by means of death, for the redemption of
the transgressions under the first covenant, *that those
who are called may receive the promise of the eternal
inheritance.*" (Heb. 9:15 NKJV)

Those who are called will receive the promise of the eternal inheritance.

"Giving thanks to the Father who has qualified us
to be partakers of the *inheritance* of the saints in the
light." (Col. 1:12 NKJV)

The Father has qualified us!

"In Him also we have obtained an inheritance... having believed, you were sealed with the Holy Spirit
of promise, *who is the guarantee of our inheritance*
until the redemption of the purchased possession, to
the praise of His glory. Therefore I also, after I heard
of your faith in the Lord Jesus and your love for all
the saints, do not cease to give thanks for you, making mention of you in my prayers: that the God of
our Lord Jesus Christ, the Father of glory, may give to
you the spirit of wisdom and revelation in the knowledge of Him, the eyes of your understanding being
enlightened; that you may know what is the hope of
His calling, *what are the riches of the glory of His
inheritance* in the saints." (Eph. 1:11-18 NKJV)

We have obtained an inheritance.

"To open their eyes, in order to turn them from darkness to light, and from the power of Satan to God, *that
they may receive* forgiveness of sins *and an inheri-*

tance among those who are sanctified by faith in Me."
(Acts 26:18 NKJV)

If you are sanctified by faith in Jesus, then you qualify as a par-
taker of the inheritance.

So as Isaac received an inheritance from his father, Abraham, so we
receive our inheritance from our Father through Jesus, our Lord.

What have we inherited from Jesus, and how do we receive it?

> "Are they not all ministering spirits sent forth to min-
> ister for those who will *inherit salvation*?" (Heb. 1:14
> NKJV)

> "In Him you also trusted, after you heard the word
> of truth, the gospel of your salvation; in whom also,
> having believed, you were sealed with the Holy Spirit
> of promise, who is the guarantee of our inheritance
> until the redemption of the purchased possession, to
> the praise of His glory." (Eph. 1:13-14 NKJV)

> "He who overcomes shall *inherit all things*, and I
> will be his God and he shall be My son." (Rev. 21:7
> NKJV)

> "Not returning evil for evil or reviling for reviling,
> but on the contrary blessing, knowing that you were
> called to this, that you may *inherit a blessing*." (1 Pet.
> 3:9 NKJV)

> "That you do not become sluggish, but imitate those
> who through faith and patience *inherit the promises*."
> (Heb. 6:12 NKJV)

"Then the King will say to those on His right hand,
'Come, you blessed of My Father, *inherit the kingdom*
prepared for you from the foundation of the world.'"
(Matt. 25:34 NKJV)

"Blessed are the meek, For they shall *inherit the
earth.*" (Matt. 5:5 NKJV)

"And everyone who has left houses or brothers or sisters or father or mother or wife or children or lands,
for My name's sake, shall receive a hundredfold, and
inherit eternal life." (Matt. 19:29 NKJV)

"That I may cause those who love me to *inherit
wealth, that I may fill their tre*asuries" (Prov. 8:21
NKJV)

"Wait on the LORD, And keep His way, And He shall
exalt you to *inherit the land*; When the wicked are cut
off, you shall see it." (Ps. 37:34 NKJV)

By reading the list of Scriptures above, we see that we inherit
from Jesus salvation and the Holy Spirit. Now the Holy Spirit is
the deposit for the rest of the inheritance. As executor of His own
testament, Jesus is able to distribute the inheritance in whatever
ways He wishes. Yet, He seems to give us this grace sometimes
according to our works.

For instance, in 1 Peter 3:9 we see that we will inherit a blessing
in return for blessing others.

"He *who overcomes* shall inherit all things." (Rev.
21:7 NKJV)

> "Blessed are *the meek* for they shall inherit the earth." (Matt. 5:5)

> "Everyone who has left houses or brothers or sisters or father or mother or wife or children or lands, for My name's sake, shall receive a hundredfold, and inherit eternal life." (Matt. 19:9 NKJV)

We have a wise God, a Father who puts our growth in character above our growth in possessions.

Paul prays that we would be able to know the fullness of our inheritance. (See Eph. 1:18.)

In Hebrews 6 we see that faith and patience, also, are needed to inherit the promises. We don't just become Christians, and then suddenly inherit everything.

Patience is needed because it takes time for the physical to manifest the spiritual.

> "You have put all things in subjection under his feet." For in that He put all in subjection under him, He left nothing that is not put under him. *But now we do not yet see all things put under him.*" (Heb. 2:8 NKJV)

Though everything has been put in subjection under Jesus' feet, we do not yet see this reality. But we are heading towards a time when it will be. The Earth will be completely under the feet of Jesus; in fact, we read in Scripture that Jesus will come and reign on Earth for a thousand years. (See Rev. 20.)

Let us also be wary that we do not fall short by not inheriting that which Jesus has for us.

Let us listen to the warnings given by Paul:

> "But if ye be led of the Spirit, ye are not under the law. Now the works of the flesh are manifest, which are these; Adultery, fornication, uncleanness, lasciviousness, Idolatry, witchcraft, hatred, variance, emulations, wrath, strife, seditions, heresies, Envyings, murders, drunkenness, revellings, and such like: of the which I tell you before, as I have also told you in time past, that *they which do such things shall not inherit the kingdom of God*" (Gal. 5:18-21).

> "Know ye not that *the unrighteous shall not inherit the kingdom of God*" (1 Cor. 6:9).

> "But with whom was he grieved forty years? was it not with them that had sinned, whose carcases fell in the wilderness? And to whom sware he that they should not enter into his rest, but to them that believed not? *So we see that they could not enter in because of unbelief*" (Heb. 3:17-19).

We started this study on the inheritance in the Book of Numbers, so let's go back there:

> "'And you shall divide the land by lot as an inheritance among your families... You shall inherit according to the tribes of your fathers. *'But if you do not drive out the inhabitants of the land from before you, then it shall be that those whom you let remain shall be irritants in your eyes and thorns in your sides*, and they shall harass you in the land where you dwell. *'Moreover it shall be that I will do to you as I thought to do to them'*" (Num. 33:54-56 NKJV).

Although the inheritance was marked out for them by lot, they had to drive out the inhabitants of the land. If they would not have driven out the inhabitants of the land, the people there would have become thorns in their sides.

Brothers and sisters, you have to fight and contend for your inheritance. Scripture says that you are to fight the good fight of faith, and that our inheritance of the promises would come through faith and patience.

I believe that the inhabitants of the land that we have to drive out are the sins that are inside of us. It is sin that stops us from inheriting the promises of God. As a result, instead of receiving a blessing, we receive punishment. When we allow sin to remain, then we are partakers of the punishment. (See Num. 33:56.) When we drive the sin out, we inherit the land. Look at how often the inheritance is given due to good character. Pride is sin; the opposite of pride is meekness. What happens to the meek? (See Matt. 5:5.)

Are you going to remain in poverty? Are you going to remain in sickness? Are you defeated?

You must fight the good fight of faith. Don't let go. Resist the devil and he will flee. The devil tries to steal your inheritance. He lies to you, and tells you that you are not worthy to receive from God.

Well, don't worry about that, for it's true that you are not worthy. You didn't need to be. It is the Lamb of God who is worthy. All you have to do is do your best and fight. Don't settle for the status quo in life. Stagnation is unworthy of the Lamb. He would rather have us hot or cold.

Paul tells us to pray, that we would understand the riches of the
glory of the inheritance. Why do we not clearly understand it?

> "These are also proverbs of Solomon, which the men
> of Hezekiah king of Judah copied out. It is the glory
> of God to conceal a thing: but the honour of kings is
> to search out a matter." (Prov. 25:1-2)

Sometimes God plays "hide and seek" with us. In other words,
He says, "If you want it, come and find it." He knows that those
who do not believe will not come looking. Those who believe
the Scriptures and have patience will look and they will find.
God typically takes each of His children and puts them through
a training program. When you have passed these tests, you will
receive more of His inheritance.

> "Blessed *is* the man that endureth temptation: for
> when he is tried, he shall receive the crown of life,
> which the *Lord hath promised* to them that love him."
> (James 1:12)

Chapter 12

Faith

That ye be not slothful, but followers of them who through faith and patience inherit the promises. (Heb. 6:12)

God has asked us not to be slothful, but followers of them who through faith and patience inherit the promises. Let us not be slothful, therefore, in understanding faith.

Faith is one of the big three subjects to be found in the Bible. These three are: faith, hope, and love, with love being the greatest. They are like the primary colors of yellow, blue, and red. All other colors are mixtures of these three. Likewise, all the subjects contained in the Bible could be said to be mixtures of these three great subjects.

> "And now abide faith, hope, love, these three; but the greatest of these is love." (1 Cor. 13:13)

King David had three mighty men, and these three topics are God's "mighty men."

Faith Is "Spiritual Money"

The simplest way I can think of to describe faith is to say that faith is spiritual money. In the physical plane when you want to buy something, you have to pay for it with money. As we discussed previously (see chapter 4), a nation's currency is in effect based on the authority that is promised by the governing bodies. (For example, British Sterling Notes are governed by the Bank of England that promises to pay the bearer of the notes.)

In the spiritual plane when you want to pray for something, you have to pay for it with faith. You need authority from the Kingdom of Heaven to present with your request, and this is the "spiritual money" that is known as faith.

The importance of faith cannot be underestimated, for the Scriptures say that it is our faith that causes us to have victory over the world, and that without faith it is impossible to please God.

> "For whatever is born of God overcomes the world. And this is the victory that has overcome the world— our faith." (1 John 5:4 NKJV)

> "But without faith it is impossible to please Him, for he who comes to God must believe that He is, and that He is a rewarder of those who diligently seek Him." (Heb. 11:6 NKJV)

When we "buy" something in prayer, we are required to state what we want, and then we must believe that we have received it.

> "And whatever things you ask in prayer, believing, you will receive." (Matt. 21:22 NKJV)

Faith is Believing

So faith is believing. Later, we will see that it is much more than simply believing. Having not yet seen the answer to a particular prayer, we have been asked by God to believe that it will happen. This belief in the unseen is faith.

> "Now faith is the substance of things hoped for, the evidence of things not seen." (Heb. 11:2)

Faith is the power to make prayer effective. This spiritual power is given to us as a gift from God and also as fruit from the presence of the Holy Spirit. (Later in this chapter we shall look into this more.)

I have often wondered why God has chosen believing to be the key to releasing power. The best answer I can think of is that in the beginning Eve chose to believe the snake in the Garden of Eden over the words of God. She chose to believe Satan rather than God. Now we are called to believe God rather than Satan before we can enter into the glorious Kingdom of Christ.

Life is a choice. Who are we going to believe, God or Satan?

Faith is a Power

I can also see that "faith" as a power is a fundamental building block of this universe.

> "By faith we understand that the worlds were framed by the word of God, so that the things which are seen were not made of things which are visible." (Heb. 11:3 NKJV)

What has not yet been appreciated by most is that we are to be children of God who possess the attributes of our Father. One of His attributes involves being creative through the autonomous power of faith.

Just as we need to be good stewards with our money, we need to be good stewards of our faith. Being good stewards over money does not prevent us from using our money as we will, for either good or selfish purposes. In the same manner God wants us to grow in power, but this growth needs to be in check with our spiritual maturity due to the autonomous nature of faith and power.

When Jesus was in the Garden of Gethsemane, He said that He could ask His Father for twelve legions of angels and that the Father would provide it for Him. Yet we also know that this would have been against the will of God. Therefore, Jesus did not ask for it, even though He knew it would have been granted if He had!

> "Or do you think that I cannot now pray to My Father, and He will provide Me with more than twelve legions of angels? How then could the Scriptures be fulfilled, that it must happen thus?" (Matt. 26:53-54)

Likewise, by faith Peter was able to stand on the water with Jesus, but one moment later, he was sinking. The will of God had not changed within that moment. What had changed was the faith that Peter possessed. So whether God wanted him to stand or sink was not the key factor in whether he stood or sank.

> "So He said, 'Come.' And when Peter had come down out of the boat, he walked on the water to go to Jesus. But when he saw that the wind was boisterous, he

was afraid; and beginning to sink he cried out, saying,
'Lord, save me!'" (Matt. 14:29-30 NKJV)

There is a neutral aspect involved with the power of faith, just as
there is with money. It can be spent for good or evil. In fact, faith
in the wrong hands can be used in witchcraft.

Sometimes when people are poor, it is not good enough just to
give them money. It is far better to teach them how to create
wealth.

In the same manner we can see from Jesus' ministry that He tried
to encourage the growth of belief/faith, rather than just using His
own faith to heal people.

> "Teacher, I brought You my son, who has a mute spir-
> it. And wherever it seizes him, it throws him down; he
> foams at the mouth, gnashes his teeth, and becomes
> rigid. So I spoke to Your disciples, that they should
> cast it out, but they could not.' He answered him and
> said, '*O faithless generation*, how long shall I be with
> you? How long shall I bear with you? Bring him to
> Me.' Then they brought him to Him. And when he
> saw Him, immediately the spirit convulsed him, and
> he fell on the ground and wallowed, foaming at the
> mouth. So He asked his father, 'How long has this
> been happening to him?' And he said, 'From child-
> hood. And often he has thrown him both into the fire
> and into the water to destroy him. But if You can do
> anything, have compassion on us and help us." Jesus
> said to him, *'If you can believe, all things are possible
> to him who believes.'* Immediately the father of the
> child cried out and said with tears, *'Lord, I believe;
> help my unbelief!'* (Mark 9:17-23 NKJV)

Many were healed by Jesus because they had faith.

> "When Jesus departed from there, two blind men fol-
> lowed Him, crying out and saying, 'Son of David,
> have mercy on us!' …. And Jesus said to them, 'Do
> you believe that I am able to do this?' They said to
> Him, 'Yes, Lord.' Then He touched their eyes, saying,
> *'According to your faith let it be to you.'* And their
> eyes were opened." (Matt. 9:27-30 NKJV)

> "And suddenly, a woman who had a flow of blood
> for twelve years came from behind and touched the
> hem of His garment. For she said to herself, 'If only
> I may touch His garment, I shall be made well.' But
> Jesus turned around, and when He saw her He said,
> 'Be of good cheer, daughter; *your faith has made you
> well.'* And the woman was made well from that hour."
> (Matt. 9:20-22 NKJV)

> "Then they came to Him, bringing a paralytic who
> was carried by four men. And when they could not
> come near Him because of the crowd, they uncov-
> ered the roof where He was. So when they had broken
> through, they let down the bed on which the paralytic
> was lying. *When Jesus saw their faith*, He said to the
> paralytic, 'Son, your sins are forgiven you.'" (Mark
> 2:3-5)

Paul learned to recognize the presence of faith.

> "And in Lystra a certain man without strength in his
> feet was sitting, a cripple from his mother's womb,
> who had never walked. This man heard Paul speak-
> ing. *Paul, observing him intently and seeing that he*

had faith to be healed, said with a loud voice, 'Stand up straight on your feet!' And he leaped and walked."
(Acts 14:8-10 NKJV)

Great Works Achieved Through Faith

In the Book of Hebrews we read about many of the great works that have been achieved through faith. The following passage discusses some of these works:
Hebrews 10:38-12:2. It would be good for your faith to study each of the people listed.

As spiritual people, we are still learning how to be like God. Jesus said that with faith no bigger than a mustard seed we will be able to move mountains, and He clearly stated that nothing is impossible for us.

> "Then Jesus answered and said, '*O faithless and perverse generation*, how long shall I be with you? How long shall I bear with you? Bring him here to Me.' And Jesus rebuked the demon, and it came out of him; and the child was cured from that very hour. Then the disciples came to Jesus privately and said, 'Why could we not cast it out?' So Jesus said to them, '*Because of your unbelief*; for assuredly, I say to you, *if you have faith as a mustard seed, you will say to this mountain, "Move from here to there," and it will move; and nothing will be impossible for you.*'"
> (Matt. 17:17-20 NKJV)

This type of faith that enables us to move mountains is not yet common to the people of God. Yet Jesus says it is possible. We see glimpses of Jesus' abilities in certain ministries, but we don't see anybody walking in the fullness of Jesus' faith—yet. Jesus demonstrated His faith by walking on water, changing water into wine, multiplying fish, great multiple healings, etc.

We have His example; now we need to find the faith.

Remember, it has taken scientists thousands of years to develop nuclear bombs, bombs of such *great power*. Before the first atomic bomb was exploded they knew it was possible, but even so it had never happened before.

Likewise, the power to move a mountain is enormous; yet we know it is possible. For us to receive great faith is obviously on God's heart. Can you hear the disappointment in Jesus' following words?

> "Nevertheless, when the Son of Man comes, *will He really find faith* on the earth?" (Luke 18:8 NKJV)

I think we should take this verse to heart, forget any negative aspects that circulate about the message of faith, and understand and obtain the faith of the Kingdom of God.

If the nuclear scientists had been so negative, they would not have found the power that ended the Second World War.

When we come to Christ, we are saved through faith. That initial deposit of faith is given to us as a gift.

> "For by grace you have been saved through faith, and that not of yourselves; it is the gift of God." (Eph. 2:8 NKJV)

The Scriptures tell us that we can grow in faith.

> "We are bound to thank God always for you, brethren,
> as it is fitting, *because your faith grows exceedingly*,
> and the love of every one of you all abounds toward
> each other." (2 Thess. 1:3 NKJV)

Apart from the initial deposit of faith, how can we obtain more?

> "There are diversities of gifts, but the same Spirit....
> But the manifestation of the Spirit is given to each
> one for the profit of all: for to one is given the word
> of wisdom through the Spirit... *to another faith* by the
> same Spirit.... But one and the same Spirit works all
> these things, *distributing to each one individually as
> He wills*." (1 Cor. 12:3-11 NKJV)

The Gift of Faith

Faith can be given by the Holy Spirit as a gift. This gift is given to the individual as a gift to the Church. I became a Christian in 1982, and since then the Lord has used me many times with the gift of faith. What seems to happen with the gift of faith is that you pray for something, which would normally be unusually hard to believe, but you simply believe it will happen.

I will give you some examples of the prayers of faith the Lord has used me to pray.

I asked the Lord to provide a friend of mine with a violin. I asked first for a very good one. Then I went back to prayer and asked for a Stradivarius. I then went back and asked for a Stradivarius that was made in Stradivarius's best year. I then went back and asked that the Lord would release to her the best Stradivarius that was made during his best year.

Within a week she told me that she had been given a Stradivarius that was made in his best year. It is priceless!

Having some friends over for dinner, I had no food except for a frozen chicken. It was as hard as a table. I asked the Lord to defrost it. Laying my hands on it, the Lord defrosted it. We saw the water drip off the chicken and it was able to be cooked. This was before the invention of microwave ovens!

Multiplying Fish

When I was a student, I had very little money. One day as I was walking home with three little fishes, I asked that the Lord to multiply the fish for me, so that I could invite friends over for meals during the weekend. On arriving home there were still only three fishes. I refused to get despondent over this, so I rang my first friend Chris to invite him over for a meal. When he arrived, I discovered that he brought a box of fish with him; he was a chef and he brought it from work. Another friend who was also called Chris said to me that he had left fish in the refrigerator for me. I now had a fridge full of fish, on each level, and I was able to invite friends over for the weekend meals.

Buying A Shop With No Money

I obtained my first shop when I had no money. I purchased it with faith. After praying for the shop, the Lord said to me that He would give it to me. I asked Him how He would do this. He said, "Do everything you can, and I will do the rest." I ended up with a three-story building, which I bought in 1989.

Arriving On Time

I was late for a particular prayer meeting. Sitting on a tube train, I wondered how I could speed up the process. I thought that I would pray specifically that when I arrived at the next tube station that my train would stop next to a platform that would have a train waiting to take me to Earl's Court. When I arrived at the next station, the train stopped next to another platform, where there was a train waiting. I jumped on the train, sat down, and asked another passenger whether the train was going to Earl's Court. "No," he said, and he explained that it was going somewhere else.

"Lord," I exclaimed, "I prayed that it would go there."

Just then the operator suddenly announced, "Would everyone on the train at platform 5 get off; it is now going to Earl's Court." Praise the Lord, I was not late for the prayer meeting.

Various Healings

I have prayed for a lady who was going blind, and she was instantly healed. Another case involved a man in a hospital, who had a lump the size of an orange that needed to be removed from his lungs. I prayed for him, and the lump completely disappeared. They had to cancel his operation!

I've seen healings come to people afflicted with arthritis, damaged legs, twisted spines, heart conditions, blood problems, and all manner of sickness and disease.

Faith also comes simply by spending time with Jesus, talking to the Holy Spirit, allowing His presence to come upon you, listening to Him, and being His friend.

When you spend time with someone, you become like them. When you allow the Holy Spirit to dwell within you, His character starts to bear fruit in your life. These elements of His character are described in Scripture as "the fruit of the spirit."

> "But the fruit of the Spirit is love, joy, peace, longsuffering, gentleness, goodness, *faith*, meekness, temperance: against such there is no law." (Gal. 5:22-23 NKJV)

Another way to receive faith is to hear God speak. This is incredibly important, and it is an effective way of growing in faith.

> "So then *faith comes by hearing*, and hearing by the word of God." (Rom. 10:17 NKJV)

I was praying one day and the Lord said to me, "Martin, do you know there is an animal that uses faith?" After a little guessing, I asked him which one it was. He told me that it was the bat.

A bat has very poor vision, so to substantiate what he cannot see, he emits a sound; the sound bounces off the objects around him, and he hears the sound coming back to him. Thus, he is able to know what he cannot see. It is a little like radar.

If we examine this process, then we can see how Hebrews11:1 and Romans 10:17 work together. Also, we can learn from the bat how to walk/fly in faith.

> "Now faith is the substance of things hoped for, the evidence of things not seen." (Heb. 11:1 NKJV)

> "So then *faith comes by hearing*, and hearing by the word of God." (Rom. 10:17 NKJV)

The bat substantiates what he cannot see by hearing.

I think there is a lot more than this to understand from Romans 10:17, however.

When you are praying for something in faith, you need to emit a signal. That signal is talking to God. When you hear the response from God, you gain faith, and this substantiates the request. Because you are hearing His response to your prayer, you are asking for His opinion, and when He gives it, it encourages you and you believe what you have heard. Faith is being transmitted to you by the responses. Thus, faith comes by hearing, and hearing by the Word of God.

Often the mistake is to pray without hearing; then, when time goes by and nothing seems to be happening, doubts can creep in. Rather, we should keep talking to God and then listen to His replies about the situation in order to gain strength through His words and receive the faith that is transmitted with His words, thereby substantiating the unseen.

The next way we can receive faith is found in the Book of Jude:

> "But you, beloved, building yourselves up on your most holy faith, praying in the Holy Spirit" (Jude 1:20 NKJV).

It is possible to build your faith simply by praying in the Holy Spirit, praying in tongues.
Have you ever asked someone to pray for you, and they've said a few words, and yet you feel nothing has really happened?

In such a case we must rely on the truth of God's Word:

"The effective, fervent prayer of a righteous man
avails much. Elijah was a man with a nature like ours,
and he prayed earnestly that it would not rain; and it
did not rain on the land for three years and six months.
And he prayed again, and the heaven gave rain, and
the earth produced its fruit" (James 5:16-18 NKJV).

Also, Jesus would sometimes pray and heal people with very
few words:

"Now when Jesus had entered Capernaum, a centurion came to Him, pleading with Him, saying, "Lord,
my servant is lying at home paralyzed, dreadfully tor-
mented." And Jesus said to him, "I will come and heal
him." The centurion answered and said, "Lord, I am
not worthy that You should come under my roof. *But
only speak a word, and my servant will be healed....*
Then Jesus said to the centurion, "Go your way; and
as you have believed, so let it be done for you." And
his servant was healed that same hour (Matt. 8:5-13
NKJV).

The answer is that few words need to be said when you have
the necessary faith. Yet so much prayer is given without faith.
In such cases the prayer may be sprinkled with a little hope, but
not faith.

This is where the verse from Jude that I alluded to earlier can
help us. We need to build our faith by praying in the Holy Spirit.
Let me give you an example. A friend of mine told me that his
wife had been separated from him, he was living in London, and
that she had been placed in a psychiatric hospital in the United
States.

This separation had lasted for some time; I believe it lasted at least eighteen months. I felt very angry about this when I realized that his wife could be taken from him with an ocean separating them. I asked him whether anyone had prayed about it. He told me that many had prayed. But on hearing this in the center of my being, I did not believe that real effective prayer had taken place. I sensed that it had been only empty prayer.

I determined that I was going to pray about it. I realized that to pray effectively I would need to have a mechanism in place to keep my praying focused until the goal was achieved. Therefore, I started by asking God to give me a burden for the needs. I then started praying in tongues and pushing against the burden I had been given. I prayed for what seemed like the whole night. The next night I slept in the lounge, so that I could pray loudly without disturbing anyone. Again I prayed for what seemed like the whole night. The third night I had been praying for about an hour or so when suddenly the burden lifted. There was no more reason to pray; I now *knew* the prayer had been answered, for I felt "light" in my spirit and I wanted to praise God. I truly knew the prayer had been answered.

Within a couple of weeks this lady had been healed, and she was back with her husband in London.

Let's take a look now at the mechanics of this prayer. When I started the session of prayer, I did not know that the prayer had been answered. If I had known the prayer was answered, there would have been no need to continue in prayer. After many hours of prayer I suddenly *knew* the prayer was answered. Something had changed; *knowing* that the prayer was answered had given me great faith. So I had *built* myself up in faith by praying in the Holy Spirit.

This progression of prayer can also be found in Philippians:

> "Be anxious for nothing, but in everything by prayer
> and supplication, with thanksgiving, let your requests
> be made known to God; and the peace of God, which
> surpasses all understanding, will guard your hearts
> and minds through Christ Jesus" (Phil. 4:6-7 NKJV).

First Stage: We Start Praying.

Second Stage: Make Supplications.

As we pray, we begin to include our supplications. Just as you can reason with your earthly father for a request, we can reason with God as to why we want Him to honor our requests. I chose to do this stage of prayer in tongues, but it can be done in your own natural language, as well. The important thing is not to go to stage three before you know the prayer has been answered. Sometimes people will suggest that you go to stage three prematurely; they will state that by thanking God you are displaying your faith.

I disagree with this because it is important for your development in prayer to *know* you have the faith. Hope alone does not make prayer work. Thanking God for the answer to a prayer when you don't yet really believe that the answer is given is premature. You don't want a premature baby, because it might die, and you don't want to prematurely thank God for what you do not yet believe, because you don't want the prayer to die.
To thank God prematurely is not appropriate, because not enough has been accomplished to enable you to achieve the desired result. Continue in prayer until your spirit bursts with joy, *knowing* the prayer is answered. If you do not know the prayer

has been answered, you do not yet have the faith for the prayer to be answered.

We can ask God for more faith, and we can ask Him to help us in our unbelief. (See Mark 9:24.)

I was once locked out of my house. Knowing that a builder who had a set of keys had been working there, I prayed that the Lord would send him around the corner immediately so I could get in with his key. I had left my clarinets in the house, and it was getting close to the time when I would be late for a rehearsal.

The Lord asked me, "Do you believe I will send him?"

I answered, "I half believe."

The Lord responded to me by saying, "I can't half send him."

What fun it is working for God. I responded to the Lord that although I only half believed He could send him, I did believe He could get me into the house. Within a minute, I was in the house.

Remember, if you only half believe, God can't "half do."

Third Stage: Giving of Thanks.

Fourth Stage: Receiving of Peace.

It seems to me that when God gives us peace after a session of prayer, our receiving of peace is God's "calling card" that the prayer request is now in His hands and has been answered.

Let us not take this process of prayer in vain, rushing through the stages without truly being respectful of the process. Failing in prayer does not encourage us or those we are praying for.

The effective, fervent prayer of the righteous man achieves much. (See James 5:16.)

Much prayer is done from a sincere heart, but sincerity alone does not bring the answer to prayer. We need effective, sincere prayer. Empty prayer, prayer that is devoid of faith, is not effective. We should not kid ourselves when we are praying for ourselves and other people by saying that we have faith when we don't really have faith. This causes disappointment, and it breeds unbelief. If you go into a BMW store and try to buy a new car but don't have enough money, you will only embarrass yourself and the salesman. In that case you will go away disappointed. If you try to give £10 for a £50,000 car, it will not be accepted simply because you don't have enough money to pay for the automobile. Don't get upset by this, for this is reality. If you do not have enough authority or money, then you will be unable to purchase the vehicle. However, you can go away and try to increase the amount of money you have to enable you to buy the car.

Likewise, if you do not have the faith to "purchase" a prayer request, you will have to go and find the faith you need. You can build up your faith by praying in the Holy Spirit.

> "Now the end of the commandment is charity out of
> a pure heart, and of a good conscience, and of faith
> unfeigned: From which some having swerved have
> turned aside unto vain jangling." (1Tim. 1:5-6)

I have another interesting example to share with you.

Around 1985 I was in a fast-food restaurant in Earl's Court in London. As I was eating my food, I became aware that the Lord wanted me to talk to one of the servers about Him.

By the time I had mustered the courage to get up and speak to him, he had disappeared into one of the back rooms. I asked the manager if he could get him so that I could speak to him. The manager asked me, "Why?"

I was a little embarrassed by his question, so I said, "Because God wants me to speak to him."

At that point the whole restaurant went quiet, or so it seemed. The manager brought the man out to me. I talked to him and found out that his name was Sunday. He wondered why God would want me to help him. He told me that he came from Ghana, and before he left for London, he had met a girl whom he had only spoken to for about a day. He felt God wanted him to marry this young lady. As it was very difficult for some to get visas to come to England, he was unsure with regard to how he should progress with his desires. I simply prayed in one or two sentences that God would bring the girl over from Ghana and be married to him.

About one month later she agreed to marry him, got a visa, crossed the ocean, and married him! I was honored to be a guest at their wedding.

Do you see how I did not have to spend days praying in tongues with regard to this prayer? My earlier intercession for my friend's wife to be reunited with her husband from across the ocean, had given me the faith to be able to pray simply, without intercession, for this lady to cross the ocean.

The Motives of Our Hearts

The next way of obtaining faith is the most important one of all. It involves the motives of our hearts.

"And the apostles said to the Lord, *'Increase our faith.'* So the Lord said, *'If you have faith as a mustard seed,* you can say to this mulberry tree, "Be pulled up by the roots and be planted in the sea," and it would obey you. And which of you, having a servant plowing or tending sheep, will say to him when he has come in from the field, 'Come at once and sit down to eat'? But will he not rather say to him, 'Prepare something for my supper, and gird yourself and serve me till I have eaten and drunk, and afterward you will eat and drink'? Does he thank that servant because he did the things that were commanded him? I think not. So likewise you, when you have done all those things which you are commanded, say, *'We are unprofitable servants.* We have done what was our duty to do.'" (Luke 17:5-10 NKJV)

The apostles wanted the Lord to increase their faith, but what was the point the Lord was making to them? I think the answer can be found in verse 10: "When you have done all those things which you are commanded, say, 'We are unprofitable servants.'"

I think the translation here is a little awkward. This may be deliberate on God's part; perhaps He wants us to dig to find a nugget. If we look in *Strong's Dictionary* for the definition of the word that is translated as "unprofitable," we find this:

888 ἀχρεῖος achreios
Meaning: 1) useless, good for nothing
Usage: AV - unprofitable

Therefore, this word could be translated as "When you have done all those things which you are commanded, say, 'We are useless servants!'"

However, this doesn't quite get to the heart of it, as it goes beyond self-deprecation. I am a useless servant. I am a good-for-nothing servant.

Yet it is possible to see clearly what Jesus was saying to the apostles:

No. 1—In response to their request to increase their faith, Jesus said that if they had faith as a mustard seed, they could . . . . Basically *when* you have the substance called faith it will easily achieve the result, which is released through talking:

> "Ye might *say* unto this sycamine tree, be thou
> plucked up by the root, and be thou planted in the sea;
> and it should obey you" (Luke 17:6).

No. 2—Having the faith is NOT the important thing. What is important is your heart attitude. Do you want to work miracles? Why? Do you want everyone to look at you while you do the miracles? Do you want to receive the praises of men when they see you do miracles?

God is not looking for showmen and magicians.
At this point the apostles' motives were not quite right. They wanted the power, but not from completely pure motives.

Faith is energized through love. Our attitude with regard to working miracles should be the compulsion that comes from compassion for the sick, the needy, and the lost.

Jesus questioned the motives of the apostles. Our attitude should be one of a useless servant. But what I really think this means is that when we perform a miracle, we should make it clear that this great power that works through us exists because we are *ser-*

vants of God and that the *use* of God's power did not come from
us. The power is not inherent in us from our own self-developed
abilities. Rather, the *use* is not from us, the power is not from us;
we are *useless* servants who are simply administering the gift of
God for the recipients through obedience.

The first time I taught on this passage of Scripture the Lord
backed up the preaching by instantly healing a man. He had been
in a motorcycle accident many years before and could not walk
properly. The Lord was gracious to him and instantly healed his
legs as I prayed for him.

It is interesting to see how Peter would try to imitate Jesus in his
faith. We can learn a great deal from this:

> "Jesus went unto them, walking on the sea. And
> when the disciples saw him walking on the sea, they
> were troubled, saying, it is a spirit; and they cried out
> for fear. But straightway Jesus spake unto them, say-
> ing, Be of good cheer; it is I; be not afraid. And Peter
> answered him and said, Lord, if it be thou, bid me
> come unto thee on the water. And he said, Come. And
> when Peter was come down out of the ship, *he walked
> on the water*, to go to Jesus. But when he saw the
> wind boisterous, he was afraid; and *beginning to sink*,
> he cried, saying, Lord, save me. And immediately Je-
> sus stretched forth his hand, and caught him, and said
> unto him, *O thou of little faith, wherefore didst thou
> doubt?*" (Matt. 14:24-31 NKJV)

As I have mentioned previously, faith is like money. Too often
we waver in our faith, using the will of God as an excuse for our
failures. The above portion of Scripture is interesting because it

shows us that the will of God remains a constant, while the effect of Peter's faith shows contrasting results.

We can see that Jesus asked Peter to come to Him on the water. Now I am fairly sure Jesus did not then change His mind and decide He would like Peter to start sinking! So what was the difference between success and failure? Jesus gives us the answer to this question: *"O thou of little faith, wherefore didst thou doubt?"*

Peter's faith was small and it was overridden by his doubts. The doubts were caused by his eyes looking at the boisterous wind and then coming to the conclusion that he would no longer be able to walk on the water.

The enemy of faith is unbelief. Unbelief is caused by doubts, anxieties, and fear.

In my life I have noticed different levels of faith at different times. Like many, the honeymoon period when you first get saved is a time of great faith. Having now been able to see the Kingdom of Heaven, it is such a great surprise when all one's friends don't immediately get saved when you tell them the truth about the Kingdom. The important thing to remember, of course, is that the individual must have faith, not necessarily his or her friends.

I would pray for unusual things because God gave me a gift of faith. Having been taught that one should step out in faith, I would look for an action for my faith. For example, if I were late for a class at the Royal Academy of Music, I would pray that I would be able to run to the end of the road and jump and that I would land on a bus that would take me to college. Not being able to see around the corner, and not knowing the bus routes,

I would set off and jump. I indeed landed on the back of a bus, the route-master busses that you have in London, which have an open, small platform on the back, which was traveling to a stop right outside my college. What laughter I would have when this would happen.

One night I was traveling on a bus that was coming back from the north of England. I really wanted a cup of coffee, but it was 1:30 in the morning. Again, in looking for an action, I asked God if He would put a cup of coffee into my hand if I closed my eyes and stuck my hand up into the air in the shape of a cup. As I closed my eyes and raised my hand, somebody put a cup of coffee into my hand. The only problem was that it did not contain sugar. Maybe I should have asked for that, as well!

The difficulty, though, is that faith, like coffee can go cold. After a while the number of miracles I saw began to fade. It was as if it would have been hard for me to pray for my coffee to be warm right after I had made it.

Why did my faith fade?

When Peter first started walking on the water, he was looking at Jesus; he started to sink when he started looking at the effects of the boisterous wind instead of looking at Jesus.

Often we can spend too much time looking at television or other attractions. If we look at those things too much or look at the wrong things, our faith will deteriorate.

Our relationship with Jesus changes as we get older. The effervescence of the honeymoon love we once had for Him changes to a stronger, trusting love that emanates from the adversities of life.

It was important for me to understand that my level of faith had been given to me as a gift. For me to understand people with different gifts and talents, I needed to see my life as a Christian without that faith. That type of faith was removed but then given back to me in a different way. I can say that my faith has gone through a maturing process with less frivolity, but it still leads me to pray for some unusually hard things.

For example, the Lord has said that He will give me a six-billion-pound skyscraper. I have had this confirmed from some other ministers, and I fully believe it will happen. He has told me that it will be used to "beam the gospel into every nation on the earth."

I think that middle-aged Christians can often fade in their faith towards God and sink into mediocrity. We need to take Paul's words to heart and press towards the high calling of God.

> "This one thing I do, forgetting those things which are behind, and reaching forth unto those things which are before, I press toward the mark for the prize of the high calling of God in Christ Jesus." (Phil. 3:13-14 NKJV)

Counterfeit Faith

In addition to unbelief, fear, doubts, anxieties, and fretting, another enemy of faith is what I call counterfeit faith.

This is a serious problem because it causes even good Christians to stop praying. They pray with counterfeit faith, and nothing happens. Their prayer is not answered, and they lose hope and stop praying.

I have on a number of occasions gone to the bank to deposit the business receipts only to find that a £20 note is a counterfeit. In such a case the note is taken from me, and then it is sent to the Bank of England. What I thought was genuine was in fact worthless. It looked correct and felt correct, but it did not carry the authority of the Bank of England; therefore, it is a worthless piece of paper.

Sometimes we pray and we genuinely believe that we are going to get the answer to the prayer and yet it doesn't happen. Why? Because it is *counterfeit* faith!

I think some of the confusion stems from the translation of words in the New Testament Greek into English.

> "Jesus answered and said unto them, Verily I say unto you, If ye have *faith*, and doubt not, ye shall not only do this which is done to the fig tree, but also if ye shall say unto this mountain, Be thou removed, and be thou cast into the sea; it shall be done. And all things, whatsoever ye shall ask in prayer, *believing*, ye shall receive." (Matt. 21:21-22)

Matthew 21:21 says, "If you have faith," yet in verse 22 it says, "believing ye shall receive."

Both the words that are translated as "faith" (4102) and "believing" (4100) come from the same root word in Greek. *Strong's Dictionary* provides us with the following definitions:

Strong's Reference no. 4102
πίστις pistis

Meaning:
1) conviction of the truth of anything, belief; in the NT of a conviction or belief respecting man's relationship to God and divine things, generally with the included idea of trust and holy fervor born of faith and joined with it
1a) relating to God 1a1) the conviction that God exists and is the creator and ruler of all things, the provider and bestower of eternal salvation through Christ
1b) relating to Christ
1b1) a strong and welcome conviction or belief that Jesus is the Messiah, through whom we obtain eternal salvation in the kingdom of God
1c) the religious beliefs of Christians
1d) belief with the predominate idea of trust (or confidence) whether in God or in Christ, springing from faith in the same
2) fidelity, faithfulness
2a) the character of one who can be relied on

Strong's Reference no. 4100
πιστεύω pisteuo

Meaning:
1) to think to be true, to be persuaded of, to credit, place confidence in
1a) of the thing believed
1a1) to credit, have confidence
1b) in a moral or religious reference
1b1) used in the NT of the conviction and trust to which a man is impelled by a certain inner and higher prerogative and law of soul

1b2) to trust in Jesus or God as able to aid either in obtaining or in doing something: saving faith
1b3) mere acknowledgment of some fact or event: intellectual faith
2) to entrust a thing to one, i.e. his fidelity
2a) to be entrusted with a thing

The reason why this is so important is that in English the word "believe" doesn't have the same strength as the word "faith."

The issue is not whether you believe something, for that doesn't mean you have faith. For example, a few hundred years ago scientists believed that the world was flat. Just because they believed it, did not make it true. Many scientists now believe we come from monkeys, but that does not make it true.

> "And all things, whatsoever ye shall ask in prayer, *believing*, ye shall receive." (Matt. 21:22)

Really this verse should say: "And all things, whatsoever ye shall ask in prayer, *in faith*, ye shall receive."

Solely having belief does not mean you have faith. It may almost look the same as faith, just as counterfeit money looks the same as real money, but there is a difference.

Real faith is a substance; it is the evidence of things not seen. This is a quality of belief that is backed up by genuine evidence and authority.

> "Now the end of the commandment is charity out of a pure heart, and of a good conscience, and of *faith unfeigned*." (1Tim. 1:5)

> "Now faith is the substance of things hoped for, the evidence of things not seen." (Heb. 11:1)

How can we tell the difference between faith and belief? Admittedly, this is difficult in the same way it is difficult to see the difference between genuine and counterfeit currency.

The main difference I would look for focuses on where you are believing? True faith comes from the heart, not from the mind.

> "For with the heart man believeth (*pisteuo*, faith) unto righteousness." (Rom. 10:10)

Do you have a real belief in the center of your being that is backed up with joy over the fact that your prayer has been answered? If you don't have the joy, then maybe the faith is just belief or hope.

Conversely, I have found that there can be a battle in the mind when you are praying in faith. This can confuse the person who is praying by leading them to think that he or she doesn't have faith and is wavering. In this situation the mind is a battlefield. Sometimes when I am praying in faith for something, in my mind I hear Satan saying, "God won't do that for you; God won't do that for you." When this happens, the devil is trying to corrupt my faith. Once the prayer has been answered, however, he usually changes his tune to: "God didn't do it, God didn't do it." I don't think his tactics have changed much through the centuries.

When you want to distinguish between faith and belief, keep talking to God. Listening to His replies will help you establish what real faith is. On many occasions I have received wonderful presents from God simply by being patient and listening to what He has to say. Sometimes He will say to me, "Wait," or "Not yet." Each time I have waited, however, I have received something much better.

Without doubt, listening to God is the best way to receive faith.

Chapter 13

Patience

> "But you, O man of God, flee these things and pursue righteousness, godliness, faith, love, patience, gentleness." (1 Tim. 6:11 NKJV)

Why have we been asked to pursue patience? What is so important about waiting? The Bible gives us a clear answer to these questions:

> "My brethren, count it all joy when you fall into various trials, knowing that the testing of your faith produces patience. But let patience have its perfect work, that you may be perfect and complete, lacking nothing" (James 1:2 NKJV).

Would you like to be perfect? Would you like to be complete? Would you like to lack nothing?

What a promise this is. The fruit of patience is perfection, wholeness, and lacking nothing!

The Scriptures also show us that patience in conjunction with well-doing brings us glory, honor, immortality, and eternal life. Patience in conjunction with faith helps us to inherit the promises of God. (See Luke 8:15; Luke 21:19; Rom. 2:7, and Heb. 6:12-15).

Hope is expressed by patience. (See 1 Thess. 1:3.) When we
hope, we are expectant. As we learn to hope, then we eagerly
wait for the answer of our hope.

"For we are saved by hope: but hope that is seen is not hope:
for what a man seeth, why doth he yet hope for? But if we hope
for that we see not, then do we with patience wait for it." (Rom.
8:24-25)

Now let us read Romans 5:1-5 very carefully because it shows
us how to obtain patience.

> "...we glory in tribulations also: knowing that tribula-
> tion worketh patience; And patience, experience; and
> experience, hope: And hope maketh not ashamed; be-
> cause the love of God is shed abroad in our hearts by
> the Holy Ghost which is given unto us." (Rom. 5:3-5)

When we are experiencing tribulation, we have no choice but to
weather it. To our souls it is comparable to a sword being heated
in the fire in an effort to strengthen it. Each time we have to go
through a tribulation we find it easier to endure, because we have
experienced tribulation before. Each time we go through tribulation God brings us safely through, so why should we worry
about the next tribulation we have to face?

In this way we are learning to be patient, to wait under pressure,
knowing God will come through on our behalf. The more experience we have of God coming through for us, the more expecta-
tion we will have of Him. In this way we find hope. Hope is like
a torch in a dark tunnel. It tells us that we will get through, that
things will change.

Now we can see why James says to count it all joy when we
encounter various trials. The testing we go through produces pa-

tience in our lives. Once we have patience, praying for things becomes easier, because we will be happy to wait for God to answer the prayers. As we mature in faith and patience we will no longer doubt every few minutes if we don't see the answer we want.

Pay attention to Solomon's wise words:

> "The end of a matter is better than its beginning, and patience is better than pride" (Eccles. 7:8).

Never forget that the end of a matter is more important than the beginning!!!!!!!

.

Chapter 14

God's Provision

"For even when we were with you, we commanded you this: If anyone will not work, neither shall he eat." (2 Thess. 3:10 NKJV)

There are many people who do not have jobs. The above commandment is not for those who cannot find work, but it is for those who don't want to work.

In *our* walk with God we should always be working for Him. There are many things we can be doing:

1. Working in full-time ministry.
2. Working in jobs so as to produce finances and being the salt of the world.
3. Helping the church, helping the pastor, etc.
4. Special ministries for the Lord, such as intercession (prayer), evangelism, etc.

Our lives should consist of a combination of the above. Notice what Jesus has to say about this: To sum up this "work" that we do, can be found in Matthew 6:33.

"Therefore I say unto you, Take no thought for your life, what ye shall eat, or what ye shall drink; nor yet for your body, what ye shall put on. Is not the life

more than meat, and the body than raiment? Behold
the fowls of the air: for they sow not, neither do they
reap, nor gather into barns; yet your heavenly Father
feedeth them. Are ye not much better than they? Which
of you by taking thought can add one cubit unto his
stature? And why take ye thought for raiment? Consider the lilies of the field, how they grow; they toil
not, neither do they spin: And yet I say unto you, That
even Solomon in all his glory was not arrayed like
one of these. Wherefore, if God so clothe the grass of
the field, which to day is, and to morrow is cast into
the oven, shall he not much more clothe you, O ye of
little faith? Therefore take no thought, saying, What
shall we eat? or, What shall we drink? or, Wherewith-
al shall we be clothed? (For after all these things do
the Gentiles seek) for your heavenly Father knoweth
that ye have need of all these things. But *seek ye first
the kingdom of God, and his righteousness*; and all
these things shall be added unto you. Take therefore
no thought for the morrow: for the morrow shall take
thought for the things of itself. Sufficient unto the day
is the evil thereof." (Matt. 6:25-34)

We see from this passage that God will provide for us in every
way, including basic physical necessities, *when we comply with
His condition* of seeking first the Kingdom of God.

"Carry neither money bag, knapsack, nor sandals;
and greet no one along the road. But whatever house
you enter, first say, 'Peace to this house.' And if a son
of peace is there, your peace will rest on it; if not, it
will return to you. And remain in the same house, eating and drinking such things as they give, for the la-
bourer is worthy of his wages. Do not go from house
to house." (Luke 10:4-7 NKJV)

When Jesus sent His disciples out to work for Him, He told them to take no money with them and no bags for food or extra shoes. It wasn't because He wanted them to be poor, but that they would know that when they were working for Him He would provide for everything. As it says in Luke 10:7, the laborer is worthy of his wages!

When you work for God, God pays!!

Notice when Jesus sent them out He did not say they did not have any money, but not to *take* a money bag with them. They must have had money bags for Jesus to say not to take them.

Let us read how God provided for the children of Israel when they were in the wilderness.

> "And when the layer of dew lifted, there, on the sur-face of the wilderness, was a small round substance, as fine as frost on the ground.   So when the children of Israel saw it, they said to one another, "What is it?" For they did not know what it was. And Moses said to them, "This is the bread which the LORD has given you to eat. "This is the thing which the LORD has commanded: 'Let every man gather it according to each one's need, one omer for each person, according to the number of persons; let every man take for those who are in his tent.'" *Then the children of Israel did so and gathered, some more, some less. So when they measured it by omers, he who gathered much had nothing left over, and he who gathered little had no lack.* ... And the house of Israel called its name Manna. And it was like white coriander seed, and the taste of it was like wafers made with honey." (Exod. 16:14-31 NKJV)

We see that some gathered a great deal, and some gathered a little bit, but all had enough.

In writing the second letter to the Corinthians, Paul mentions this passage when he says that our abundance provides for others' lack, and their abundance provides for our lack.

> "For if there is first a willing mind, it is accepted according to what one has, and not according to what he does not have. For I do not mean that others should be eased and you burdened; but by an equality, that now at this time your abundance may supply their lack, that their abundance also may supply your lack— that there may be equality. As it is written, "He who gathered much had nothing left over, and he who gathered little had no lack." (2 Cor. 8:12-15 NKJV)

So we see that when God provides for us, it is not just for ourselves but for others also.

> "Give, and it will be given to you: good measure, pressed down, shaken together, and running over will be put into your bosom. For with the same measure that you use, it will be measured back to you." (Luke 6:38 NKJV)

The Bible says that when we give, it is like sowing a seed into the ground. When we sow a little, we get a little back; when we sow bountifully, we shall reap bountifully.

> "But this I say: He who sows sparingly will also reap sparingly, and he who sows bountifully will also reap bountifully. So let each one give as he purposes in his heart, not grudgingly or of necessity; for God loves

a cheerful giver. And God is able to make all grace abound toward you, that you, always having all sufficiency in all things, may have an abundance for every good work." (2 Cor. 9:6-8 NKJV)

God Loves a Cheerful Giver

God provides for the Church—its upkeep, wages for ministers and musicians, and other needs through the system of tithes.

> "Bring all the tithes into the storehouse, That there may be food in My house, And try Me now in this," Says the LORD of hosts, "If I will not open for you the windows of heaven And pour out for you such blessing That there will not be room enough to receive it." (Mal. 3:10 NKJV)

When we don't tithe, we rob God and His provision for the Church:

> "Will a man rob God? Yet you have robbed Me! But you say, 'In what way have we robbed You?' In tithes and offerings" (Mal. 3:8 NKJV).

When we tithe, God promises to bless us:

> "Bring all the tithes into the storehouse, That there may be food in My house, And try Me now in this," Says the LORD of hosts, "If I will not open for you the windows of heaven And pour out for you such blessing That there will not be room enough to receive it" (Mal. 3:10 NKJV).

Let us remember that God wants us to prosper! Note the next two verses:

> "Beloved, I wish above all things that thou mayest prosper and be in health, even as thy soul prospereth" (3 John 1:2).

> "Let them shout for joy, and be glad, that favour my righteous cause: yea, let them say continually, Let the LORD be magnified, which hath pleasure in the prosperity of his servant" (Ps. 35:27).

When we give, God is pleased with us. He wants us to be cheerful givers, and He wants us to prosper.

When we give, it is not according to how much we give, but according to our heart and our ability.

> "And Jesus sat over against the treasury, and beheld how the people cast money into the treasury: and many that were rich cast in much. And there came a certain poor widow, and she threw in two mites, which make a farthing. And he called unto him his disciples, and saith unto them, Verily I say unto you, That this poor widow hath cast more in, than all they which have cast into the treasury: For all they did cast in of their abundance; but she of her want did cast in all that she had, even all her living." (Mark 12:41-44)

When the poor widow put two mites into the offering, Jesus said she had given more than all the rich people had.

"Finally let us remember the exhortation that God gave to Abraham: "Saying, Surely blessing I will bless thee, and multiplying I will multiply thee." (Heb. 6:14)

God wants us to be blessed, and He wants us to be prosperous, but not just for ourselves; we are to reach out to others and to the Church, as well.

Let us remember what God has given to us:

"For God so loved the world, that he gave his only begotten Son, that whosoever believeth in him should not perish, but have everlasting life" (John 3:16).

Chapter 15

Poverty and Our Debt to the Poor

One of the benefits of being poor is that it is easier to *enter* the Kingdom of God in that state.

The Bible teaches us that it is hard for a rich man to enter the Kingdom of God. Often, the rich do not see their need for God. Yet once we are living in the Kingdom of God we find that it is God's will to prosper us. We even find out that Jesus became poor so that we could be rich!!

> "Then said Jesus unto his disciples, Verily I say unto you, That a rich man shall hardly enter into the kingdom of heaven. And again I say unto you, It is easier for a camel to go through the eye of a needle, than for a rich man to enter into the kingdom of God." (Matt. 19:23-24)

> "Beloved, I wish above all things that thou mayest prosper and be in health, even as thy soul prospereth." (3 John 1:2)

> "For ye know the grace of our Lord Jesus Christ, that, though he was rich, yet for your sakes he became

poor, that ye through his poverty might be rich." (2
Cor. 8:9)

When God prospers us, we then have a responsibility toward the
poor. It is not good enough just to pray for the poor; you must
feed them, as well.

When God destroyed Sodom, many people think that He did
so only because of their sexual immorality. However, Ezekiel
16:49 says this:

> "Behold, this was the iniquity of thy sister Sodom,
> pride, fullness of bread, and abundance of idleness
> was in her and in her daughters, *neither did she
> strengthen the hand of the poor and needy.*"

God destroyed Sodom because of the people's pride; having a
fullness of bread, *they would not strengthen the hand of the poor
and needy.*

Our faith must communicate more than just words.

What is Poverty?

> "Moreover all these curses shall come upon thee, and
> shall pursue thee, and overtake thee, till thou be de-
> stroyed; *because thou hearkenedst not unto the voice
> of the LORD thy God, to keep his commandments and
> his statutes which he commanded thee....* Therefore
> shalt thou serve thine enemies which the LORD shall
> send against thee, in hunger, and in thirst, and in na-
> kedness, *and in want of all things*: (Deut. 28:45-48)

In this part of the Bible God is explaining to the children of Israel that they had a choice either to obey God and be blessed, or to disobey Him and be cursed.

We can clearly see that poverty is a curse, not a blessing.

In verse 48 we see four different aspects of poverty: hunger, thirst, nakedness, and want of all things.

When we have a "want of ALL things," we find that even our neighbors don't want to know us.

People who have severe needs are not always attractive to other people, often because their neediness is generally very visible. The opposite is also true, that rich people will always have many friends. (See Prov. 14:20 & 19:4.)

We know that poverty ultimately comes from God when we make the choice to disobey Him, but how else can we be responsible for it?

1. Wickedness brings poverty:

> "The righteous eateth to the satisfying of his soul: but the belly of the wicked shall want" (Prov. 13:25).

> "The LORD maketh poor, and maketh rich: he bringeth low, and lifteth up" (1 Sam. 2:7).

2. Lack of Wisdom, brings poverty:

> "The lips of the righteous feed many: but fools die for want of wisdom" (Prov. 10:21).

3. If you refuse God's teaching and refuse His instructions, your foolishness will bring you to poverty:

"Poverty and shame shall be to him that refuseth instruction: but he that regardeth reproof shall be honoured" (Prov. 13:18).

4. Laziness and sleeping too much will bring you poverty:

"How long wilt thou sleep, O sluggard? when wilt thou arise out of thy sleep? Yet a little sleep, a little slumber, a little folding of the hands to sleep: So shall thy poverty come as one that travelleth, and thy want as an armed man" (Prov. 6:9-11).

5. Too much attention to your own pleasures, drinking, eating, etc. will bring you to poverty:

"He that loveth pleasure shall be a poor man: he that loveth wine and oil shall not be rich" (Prov. 21:17).

6. When you try and force riches, seeking first your own wealth, you will come to poverty:

"He that hasteth to be rich hath an evil eye, and considereth not that poverty shall come upon him" (Prov. 28:22).

7. Make sure you diligently do your work; don't waste your time by following empty philosophers, or you will have poverty:

"He that tilleth his land shall have plenty of bread: but he that followeth after vain persons shall have poverty enough" (Prov. 28:19).

Cry out to God, fear Him, and trust Him, and He will deliver you.

> "This poor man cried, and the LORD heard him, and saved him out of all his troubles. The angel of the LORD encampeth round about them that fear him, and delivereth them. O taste and see that the LORD is good: blessed is the man that trusteth in him. O fear the LORD, ye his saints: for there is no want to them that fear him. The young lions do lack, and suffer hunger: but they that seek the LORD shall not want any good thing." (Ps. 34:6-10)

It is God who sends both poverty and wealth; He humbles and He exalts. (See 1 Sam. 2:7.)

Even though God sends poverty as a means of correction, He still loves the poor and desires to help them. He maintains their rights. (See Ps. 140:12.)

The poor and the mighty are to be treated the same.

> "My brethren, have not the faith of our Lord Jesus Christ, the Lord of glory, with respect of persons. For if there come unto your assembly a man with a gold ring, in goodly apparel, and there come in also a poor man in vile raiment; And ye have respect to him that weareth the gay clothing, and say unto him, Sit thou here in a good place; and say to the poor, Stand thou there, or sit here under my footstool: Are ye not then partial in yourselves, and are become judges of evil thoughts? (James 2:1-4)

We see the use of correction in Amos 4:7, where the Lord withheld rain from the people, yet they still would not return to Him.

"And *also I have withholden the rain from you...*
yet have ye not returned unto me, saith the LORD."
(Amos 4:7)

In the Parable of the Prodigal Son, it was the famine that helped
him to come back to his father.

"And when he had spent all, *there arose a mighty famine* in that
land; and he began to be in want. And he went and joined himself to a citizen of that country; and he sent him into his fields
to feed swine. And he would fain have filled his belly with the
husks that the swine did eat: and no man gave unto him. And
when he came to himself, he said, How many hired servants of
my father's have bread enough and to spare, and I perish with
hunger! *I will arise and go to my father, and will say unto him,
Father, I have sinned against heaven, and before thee."* (Luke
15:13-18)

When Jesus came, He was given an anointing to preach the good
news to the poor.

> "The Spirit of the Lord is upon me, because he hath
> anointed me to preach the gospel to the poor; he hath
> sent me to heal the brokenhearted, to preach deliver-
> ance to the captives, and recovering of sight to the
> blind, to set at liberty them that are bruised." (Luke
> 4:18)

Jesus also demonstrated God's love for us when He became poor
for us in order to help us.

> "For ye know the grace of our Lord Jesus Christ, that,
> *though he was rich, yet for your sakes he became
> poor, that ye through his poverty might be rich."* (2
> *Cor. 8:9)*

God is very interested in helping the poor; let us now see what He has commanded us to do for them.

> "*Defend the poor* and fatherless: do justice to the afflicted and needy." (Ps. 82:3)

> "*He that hath pity upon the poor lendeth unto the LORD*; and that which he hath given will he pay him again." (Prov. 19:17)

> "And *if thy brother be waxen poor*, and fallen in decay with thee; then *thou shalt relieve him*: yea, though he be a stranger, or a sojourner; that he may live with thee." (Lev. 25:35.

If we want to honor God, then He has said that we should have mercy on the poor.

> "He that oppresseth the poor reproacheth his Maker: but he that honoureth him *hath mercy on the poor.*" (Prov. 14:30-31)

Through the Church God has provided for us, in that we should be dependent on one another, as His children and brothers and sisters in Christ.

If we don't fulfil our duty to help the poor, we will attract curses of our own.

> "Whoso stoppeth his ears at the cry of the poor, *he also shall cry himself, but shall not be heard.*" (Prov. 21:13)

"He that giveth unto the poor shall not lack: but *he that hideth his eyes shall have many a curse.*" (Prov. 28:27)

When we fulfil our obligations to the poor, God will bless us.

"He that hath a bountiful eye *shall be blessed*; for he giveth of his bread to the poor." (Prov. 22:9)

"Then Jesus beholding him loved him, and said unto him, One thing thou lackest: go thy way, sell whatsoever thou hast, and give to the poor, and *thou shalt have treasure in heaven*: and come, take up the cross, and follow me." (Mark 10:21)

"Blessed is he that considereth the poor: the LORD will deliver him in time of trouble. The LORD will preserve him, and keep him alive; and he shall be blessed upon the earth: and thou wilt not deliver him unto the will of his enemies." (Ps. 41:1-2)

In addition to helping the poor, we should fast. Fasting not only helps us to empathize with the poor, but it also brings us spiritual power to loose bands of wickedness, undo heavy burdens, let the oppressed go free, and break every yoke. (See Isa. 58:6-12.)

By obeying God's commands to us with regard to the poor, He will surely bless us.

"Praise ye the LORD. Blessed is the man that feareth the LORD, that delighteth greatly in his commandments. His seed shall be mighty upon earth: the generation of the upright shall be blessed. Wealth and riches shall be in his house: and his righteousness endureth for ever. Unto the upright there ariseth light in the darkness: he is gracious, and full of compassion, and righteous. A good man showeth favour, and lendeth: he will guide his affairs with discretion. Surely he shall not be moved for ever: the righteous shall be in everlasting remembrance. He shall not be afraid of evil tidings: his heart is fixed, trusting in the LORD. His heart is established, he shall not be afraid, until he see his desire upon his enemies. *He hath dispersed, he hath given to the poor*; his righteousness endureth for ever; his horn shall be exalted with honour." (Ps. 112:1)

Chapter 16

Borrowing, Debts, and How to Get Out of Debt

"Owe no man any thing, but to love one another: for he
that loveth another hath fulfilled the law." (Rom. 13:8)

One might think that this verse teaches us that one is not allowed
to borrow. In the light of the Scriptures below, however, we can
see that God does at times allow us to borrow.

"If there be among you a poor man of one of thy
brethren within any of thy gates in thy land which
the LORD thy God giveth thee, thou shalt not harden
thine heart, nor shut thine hand from thy poor brother:
But thou shalt open thine hand wide unto him, and
shalt *surely lend him sufficient for his need*, in that
which he wanteth." (Deut. 15:6-8)

God would not ask us to lend to our brothers if borrowing was
wrong.

Why, then, does Romans 13:8 say that we should owe no man
any thing?

It seems to me that it means we should not withhold what we
contract to do.

For example, if we have a mortgage, we should keep up with the payments. If we have borrowed money from somebody, we should pay them back in the manner we agreed to.

When we don't pay back what we owe, we often receive curses in our lives. These curses can prevent us from getting on with our lives. We can be working hard, yet never have enough to pay our bills. We can be tithing and giving our offerings, yet we find we still do not have enough. If this is the case in your life, you need to ask, "Is there a curse operating in my life?" If so, it is time to do some weeding. (See Chapter 17.)

The Scripture says:

> "Give, and it shall be given unto you; good measure, pressed down, and shaken together, and running over, shall men give into your bosom. For with the same measure that ye mete withal it shall be measured to you again" (Luke 6:38).

Normally we look at this verse with regard to giving someone something positive. But if you have given a person negative money, by borrowing from them and not paying it back, then the same will be given back to you. You will reap "negative money," good measure, pressed down, shaken together, and running over.

In other words, you reap what you sow.

These debts need to be dealt with. It is no good just saying to God that you repent. You have to pay back the debt in order to stop it from affecting your life negatively. Indeed, it is the right thing to do. When you don't know how to contact somebody in order to return their money, I suggest that you ask the Lord what to do and make a donation to a ministry or to whomever the Lord directs.

Sometimes people can get into debt through no fault of their own. This situation might be due to a financial recession in their country, which prevents them from earning a living.

Be assured that God is aware of these things, and He will help you restore your life if you are honest and you are endeavoring to do what He says.

Steps to get out of debt:

1. Pray and ask God to give you a plan to get out of debt.

2. Find a wise man or woman who can go through your financial affairs with you. This advisor should be a Christian who can help you turn your life around. Look for someone who is already successful, someone who will genuinely help you. Don't look for money from them! But look for wisdom and have a willingness to be accountable to them as you make progress. It is sometimes possible to find Christian debt counselors who may even be able to negotiate some of your debts away. However, it is best to pay everything back and to be honorable in every area of your finances.

3. Make a list of everybody you owe money to, and start paying them back.

4. Make *absolutely sure* that you give tithes of all your income. Don't make excuses and say, "Oh, this was a gift." Tithe *everything* that comes to you.

> "Honour the LORD with thy substance, and with the firstfruits of all thine increase: So shall thy barns be filled with plenty, and thy presses shall burst out with new wine. My son, despise not the chastening of the LORD; neither be weary of his correction." (Prov. 3:9-11)

5   Make sure you are living righteously, and ask the Holy Spirit to convict you of any sin. As He does so, be sure to repent.

6   Increase your giving. Look for things in your house that you do not need, and give them away. Through giving you will unblock the blockages to your receiving.

7   Obedience. Ask God what He wants you to do. If you are finding it hard to hear, ask yourself this question: What was the last thing God asked me to do? Often we can become hard of hearing when we simply don't do the last thing asked of us. Remember what it is was and do it!

8   Work hard. Make sacrifices and give.

Be successful and seek first the Kingdom of God. (See Matt. 6:33.)

Chapter 17

My Garden

Those of you who know me will be very surprised that I am writing about my garden. (I don't like gardening.)

I do like using a garden and looking at a garden, but I always feel that I have something more important to do than gardening.

Perhaps this is symptomatic of the way we run our lives. I say this because when I talk about my garden, I am using it as a picture of my life.

God put Adam in the Garden of Eden, and his job was to tend it.

Primarily that is the job we all have—to tend our gardens.

We plant blessings in our life, and we plant curses in our lives.

What is growing in your life? Are they blessings, or are they curses that are sucking the life out of you? Very often, it may be both.

The blessings are like fruit trees, and the curses are like weeds, nettles, and thorns.

When you give, it is given back to you.

"Give, and it will be given to you: good measure, pressed down, shaken together, and running over will be put into your bosom. For with the same measure that you use, it will be measured back to you." (Luke 6:38 NKJV)

In my garden, I have a number of interesting trees. I have a motorbike tree, a watch tree, a helps tree, a television tree, a car tree, a thousand-pound note tree, etc.

When you give, it is like a farmer sowing seed into his field. The seed grows and multiplies.

As I have sown the items I mention above by giving them away, they come back to me in seasons.

One night the Lord woke me up and said that He had something important for me to do. I asked what it was, and He said that He wanted me to give a thousand pounds to another Christian brother. Well, at that time my business was under a lot of pressure, I had around four thousand pounds in the bank, but I had to pay out that week about six thousand pounds.

I had the money, but! The next morning I told my wife, who supported me, by saying, "If the Lord has said it, we had better do it." She's a good wife. We gave the money and the business survived. Now, every so often, somebody sends me a thousand pounds. This had never happened to me before. Nobody had ever given me money in those quantities before, but now suddenly I was receiving thousands of pounds from different sources. In total I have been given £48,000 since that day. Every now and again somebody would send me a thousand pounds.

I gave a £600 Gucci watch to someone who was down and out, and I received back a watch that was worth £1600.

I like this garden.

Please don't see this as just a means of getting things; however, it shows how the mechanics of sowing and reaping works. If you ask a farmer if he expects to receive something back by sowing into the ground, he would think you were mad. If you then said that he must be greedy by understanding how it works and applying it, he would doubly think you are mad.

You can be greedy with or without material wealth. A Christian's heart is judged by how he gives, not by how he receives.

As Paul said:

> "But this I say: He who sows sparingly will also reap sparingly, and he who sows bountifully will also reap bountifully. So let each one give as he purposes in his heart, not grudgingly or of necessity; for God loves a cheerful giver. And God is able to make all grace abound toward you, that you, always having all sufficiency in all things, may have an abundance for every good work" (2 Cor. 9:6-8).

Having seen that it worked, I decided that I would deliberately plant seeds in my garden.

First, I decided to plant a row of £100 bushes. I thought that the ground it was sown into would also be important. Better to sow into people and ministries who are in need, rather than simply giving to the rich. Also, I wanted to see how long it took for some seeds to prosper into fruit.

I gave a £100 to Rev. Hugh Osgood at Cornerstone Ministries. I asked that it be put towards going out for a meal, or anything else. The next day a member of Hugh Osgood's church, knowing nothing of "my gift," sent me £100 to use for my ministry. I had never received anything from anyone at Hugh's church before.

Was this a coincidence?

Now let's look at the more serious aspect of tending your garden.

Have you weeds, nettles, or thorns in your garden?

When you give, you receive back the good things. However, you also receive back the negative things.

Do you owe money to somebody? That can be like a tree bearing negative money in your life. Do you always have less money than you need? Do you wonder why you work hard, yet it's like having holes in your pockets.

The reason is that you have a big weed in your garden, and it is sucking money out of your life. Get rid of it!

Do some weeding. Weed out the debts, and pay them back. Don't solely ask God to forgive you, because you are still reaping the consequences.

True repentance is more than just saying "I'm sorry" to God. You need to make restitution.

Not only can we have weeds sucking the life out of the ground, but we can also have thorns that cause us pain.

Let us see what Jesus said about the thorns in the Parable of the Sowing of the Word.

"Now these are the ones sown among thorns; they are the ones who hear the word, "and the cares of this world, the deceitfulness of riches, and the desires for other things entering in choke the word, and it becomes unfruitful." (Mark 4:18-19)

Your garden can become unfruitful as a result of having cares in your life. Worry and anxieties only cause harm.

Root out all worries, and cares.

"*Be anxious for nothing*, but in everything by prayer and supplication, with thanksgiving, let your requests be made known to God; and the peace of God, which surpasses all understanding, will guard your hearts and minds through Christ Jesus." (Phil. 4:6-7 NKJV)

"But seek first the kingdom of God and His righteousness, and all these things shall be added to you. "Therefore *do not worry about tomorrow*, for tomorrow will worry about its own things. Sufficient for the day is its own trouble." (Matt. 6:33-34 NKJV).

"Therefore humble yourselves under the mighty hand of God, that He may exalt you in due time, *casting all your care upon Him*, for He cares for you." (1 Pet. 5:6-7 NKJV)

When you do your gardening and weeding, pull up every worry and anxiety you can find.

Be systematic and if necessary, do it daily.

The Deceitfulness of Riches—Thorns

Let's make this point as clear as possible—riches are fine. In fact, Jesus died to receive riches.

> "As for every man to whom God has given riches and wealth, and given him power to eat of it, to receive his heritage and rejoice in his labor—this *is* the gift of God." (Eccles. 5:19 NKJV)

> "Worthy is the Lamb who was slain to receive power and riches and wisdom, And strength and honor and glory and blessing!" (Rev. 5:12 NKJV)

What is not fine, however, is the worship of riches; this is described by Jesus as serving mammon.

> "No one can serve two masters; for either he will hate the one and love the other, or else he will be loyal to the one and despise the other. You cannot serve God and mammon." (Matt. 6:24 NKJV)

Seeking riches first is not the way of the Kingdom. You need to seek first the Kingdom of God and his righteousness. (See Matt. 6:33.)

> "Men of corrupt minds and destitute of the truth, who suppose that godliness is a *means of* gain. From such withdraw yourself. Now godliness with contentment is great gain." (1 Tim. 6:5-6 NKJV)

Godliness is a means of great gain, but is not to be used solely for gain. God is not mocked; you can only serve one master.

Desires for other things entering in choke the Word, and it becomes unfruitful. These are the thorns.

Strong desires, when they become greater than is morally acceptable, are described as *lusts*.

When you focus too much on a desire, there does not leave much room for focusing on what Jesus wants you to do and be. Therefore, desires which can be quite innocent in normal strength become distorted into negative forces. All too often our lives are being spent on vanity, and the time and force that are spent in pursuing vanities should be used for building God's kingdom. It is too easy to get sidetracked into the following of an idol, such as the pursuit of riches.

James puts it this way:

> "From whence come wars and fightings among you? come they not hence, even of your lusts that war in your members? Ye lust, and have not: ye kill, and desire to have, and cannot obtain: ye fight and war, yet ye have not, because ye ask not. Ye ask, and receive not, because ye ask amiss, that ye may consume it upon your lusts" (James 4:1-3).

Even our prayer can be contaminated through lusts!

Are your desires the desires God wants you to have? Are your ambitions, Gods' ambitions? If you are not sure, take them to the cross. Leave them there until God tells you to take them up.

What is growing in your garden? Is it blessings or curses?

Chapter 18

Keys to Prosperity, Good Provision, and Success

These keys are for those who want to keep an eye on their lives and want to grow in their ability to help build God's kingdom.

Keys to Prosperity

1. Be obedient to God. Be used by God to build HIS Kingdom. Listen and Obey. (See Gen. 26:4-5.)
2. Keep clean hands. Do not Sin. Forgive others. Break any curses. (See Prov. 15:6.)
3. Fear the Lord. (See Prov. 22:4.)
4. Seek first the Kingdom of God. (See Matt. 6:33.)
5. Give to God. Through tithes and offerings. God's church and kingdom are important to Him. Be a good citizen. God will respect you for it and reward you. (See Mal. 3:10.)
6. Give to the poor. When you give to the poor, you are lending to the Lord. (See Prov. 19:17.)
7. Obtain wisdom and knowledge. Read the Bible and DO what it says.
8. Work hard, be diligent, and never be lazy. (See Prov. 11:4.)
9. Take your time to make wise plans; don't rush into things. (See Prov. 21:5.)
10. Be careful about what you say. (See Prov. 18:21.)
11. Pay back ALL Debts. (See Luke 6:38.)

12. Have a balanced lifestyle. Don't be excessive in wine, food, etc. (See Prov. 23:21.)
13. Be patient and have faith. (See Heb. 6:12.)

Keys to Poverty

1. Be disobedient to God, and refuse correction. (See Prov. 13:18.)
2. Dishonor your parents. (See Deut. 5:16.)
3. Do wickedness. (See Prov. 13:25.)
4. Do not fear the Lord. (See Prov. 22:4.)
5. Put seeking pleasure as the highest priority in your life. (See Prov. 21:17.)
6. Rob God of His tithes and offerings. (See Mal. 3:8.)
7. Do not help the poor; always look after "number one." (See Prov. 21:13.)
8. Be foolish and despise wisdom. (See Prov. 10:21.)
9. Be lazy, and stay in bed a little while longer. (See Prov. 6:9-11.)
10. Rush into things, and be hasty. (See Prov. 21:5.)
11. Speak whatever comes into your mind. It will usually contain some form of sin and curses. (See Prov. 10:19.)
12. Borrow from others; don't pay them back. (See Luke 6:38.)
13. Be a drunk and a glutton. (See Prov. 23:21.)
14. Hasten after riches (for the Kingdom's sake, of course). (See Prov. 28:22.)

Chapter 19

Summary

Having read this far through this book you must be serious about prospering. The Scriptures are clear; God wants His children to prosper, even as their soul prospers. I sincerely hope that you take the admonition to heart to be doers of the word, and not just hearers, desiring the pure milk of the word, and growing.

At this point in time, I am forty-eight years old, the Lord has given me just about everything I have ever wanted, and I have tried my best to give Him everything He has wanted from me.

There is nothing like working for God, no fulfilment to be compared with working for the King of Kings.

He is able to make all grace abound toward you; that you always having all sufficiency in all things, may abound to every good work.

So press on toward the mark for your prize in the high calling of God in Christ Jesus.

> "Beloved, I wish above all things that thou mayest prosper and be in health, even as thy soul prospereth."
> (3 John 1:2)

> "But be ye doers of the word, and not hearers only, deceiving your own selves. For if any be a hearer of

the word, and not a doer, he is like unto a man beholding his natural face in a glass." (James 1:22-23)

"As newborn babes, desire the sincere milk of the
word, that ye may grow thereby." (1 Pet. 2:2)

"And God *is* able to make all grace abound toward
you; that ye, always having all sufficiency in all
things, may abound to every good work." (2 Cor. 9:8)

"I press toward the mark for the prize of the high calling of God in Christ Jesus." (Phil. 3:14)

Chapter 20

Glossary

Definitions of Hebrew, Aramaic and Greek words for prosperity from Strong's Exhaustive Concordance of the Bible

Strong's Reference No. 06743

צָלַח - tsalach

1)   to rush
2)   to advance, prosper, make progress, succeed, be profitable
2a)   to prosper
2b)   to make prosperous, bring to successful issue, cause to prosper
2b2)   to show or experience prosperity, prosper

Sample scriptures using *tsalach*:

> "The keeper of the prison looked not to anything that was under his hand; because the LORD was with him, and that which he did, the LORD made it to *prosper*" (Gen. 39:23).

"This book of the law shall not depart out of thy mouth; but thou shalt meditate therein day and night, that thou mayest observe to do according to all that is written therein: for then thou shalt make thy way *prosperous*, and then thou shalt have good success" (Josh. 1:8).

Strong's Reference No. 02896

טוֹב - towb

1) good, pleasant, agreeable
1a) pleasant, agreeable (to the senses)
1b) pleasant (to the higher nature)
1c) good, excellent (of its kind)
1d) good, rich, valuable in estimation
1e) good, appropriate, becoming
1f) better (comparative)
1g) glad, happy, prosperous (of man's sensuous nature)
1h) good understanding (of man's intellectual nature)
1i) good, kind, benign
1j) good, right (ethical) n m
2) a good thing, benefit, welfare
2a) welfare, prosperity, happiness
2b) good things (collective)
2c) good, benefit
2d) moral good n f
3) welfare, benefit, good things
3a) welfare, prosperity, happiness
3b) good things (collective)
3c) bounty

Sample Scriptures using *towb*:

I have included this verse for "towb," which is translated as "good," as it gives a good understanding as to how God uses the word.

> "And God saw the light, that it was good: and God divided the light from the darkness." (Gen. 1:4)

> "Howbeit I believed not the words, until I came, and mine eyes had seen it: and, behold, the half was not told me: thy wisdom and prosperity exceedeth the fame which I heard." (1 Kings 10:7)

> "Cry yet, saying, Thus saith the LORD of hosts; My cities through prosperity shall yet be spread abroad; and the LORD shall yet comfort Zion, and shall yet choose Jerusalem." (Zech. 1:17)

Strong's Reference No. 07965

שָׁלוֹם - shalowm

1) completeness, soundness, welfare, peace
1a) completeness (in number)
1b) safety, soundness (in body)
1c) welfare, health, prosperity
1d) peace, quiet, tranquility, contentment
1e) peace, friendship
1e1) of human relationships
1e2) with God especially in covenant relationship
1f) peace (from war)
1g) peace (as adjective)

Sample Scriptures using *shalowm*:

"Let them shout for joy, and be glad, that favour my righteous cause: yea, let them say continually, Let the LORD be magnified, which hath pleasure in the *prosperity* of his servant" (Ps. 35:27).

"And thus you shall say to him who lives *in prosperity:* 'Peace be to you, peace to your house, and peace to all that you have!" (1 Sam. 25:6 NKJV)

Strong's Reference No. 06744

צָלַח - tslach (Aramaic)

1) to prosper
1a) (Aphel) 1a1) to cause to prosper
1a2) show prosperity, be prosperous, have success, be successful

Sample Scripture using *tslach*:

"Be it known unto the king, that we went into the province of Judea, to the house of the great God, which is builded with great stones, and timber is laid in the walls, and this work goeth fast on, and prospereth in their hands" (Ezra 5:8).

Strong's Reference No. 07999

שָׁלַם – shalam

1) to be in a covenant of peace, be at peace
1a) (Qal) 1a1) to be at peace
1a2) peaceful one (participle)
1b) (Pual) one in covenant of peace (participle)

1c) (Hiphil) 1c1) to make peace with
1c2) to cause to be at peace
1d) (Hophal) to live in peace
2) to be complete, be sound
2a) (Qal) 2a1) to be complete, be finished, be ended
2a2) to be sound, be uninjured
2b) (Piel) 2b1) to complete, finish
2b2) to make safe
2b3) to make whole or good, restore, make compensation
2b4) to make good, pay
2b5) to requite, recompense, reward
2c) (Pual) 2c1) to be performed
2c2) to be repaid, be requited
2d) (Hiphil)
2d1) to complete, perform
2d2) to make an end of

Sample Scripture using *shalam*:

> "If thou wert pure and upright; surely now he would
> awake for thee, and make the habitation of thy righ-
> teousness prosperous. Though thy beginning was
> small, yet thy latter end should greatly increase" (Job
> 8:6).

Strong's Reference No. 07951

שָׁלָה - shalah

1) to be at rest, prosper, be quiet, be at ease
1a) (Qal) 1a1) to be or have quiet
1a2) to be at ease, prosper

Sample scripture using *shalah*:

> "Pray for the peace of Jerusalem: they shall prosper
> that love thee. Peace be within thy walls, and prosper-
> ity within thy palaces" (Ps. 122:6).

Strong's Reference No. 07959

שַׁלְוָה - shelev

1) ease, prosperity

Sample scripture using *shelev*:

> "And in my prosperity I said, I shall never be moved"
> (Ps. 30:6).

Strong's Reference No. 07961

שָׁלֵו – shalev

1) quiet, at ease, prosperous
1a) at ease (of persons)
1b) quiet (of land)
1c) quiet, ease
1d) ease (subst)

Sample scripture using *shalev*:

> "Behold, these *are* the ungodly, who prosper in the
> world; they increase *in* riches" (Ps. 73:12).

Strong's Reference No. 07962

שַׁלְוָה - shalvah

1) quietness, ease, prosperity

Sample Scriptures using *shalvah*:

> "Pray for the peace of Jerusalem: they shall prosper
> that love thee. Peace be within thy walls, *and* prosper-
> ity within thy palaces" (Ps. 122:6).

> "In the day of prosperity be joyful, but in the day of
> adversity consider: God also hath set the one over
> against the other, to the end that man should find
> nothing after him" (Eccles. 7:14).

Strong's Reference No. 03787

כָּשֵׁר – kasher

1) to succeed, please, be suitable, be proper, be advantageous, be
right and proper to
1a) (Qal) to please, be proper
1b) (Hiphil) to give success

Sample scripture using *kasher*:

> "In the morning sow thy seed, and in the evening
> withhold not thine hand: for thou knowest not wheth-
> er shall prosper, either this or that, or whether they
> both *shall be* alike good" (Eccles. 11:6).

Strong's Reference No. 2137

εὐοδόω euodoo

1) to grant a prosperous and expeditious journey, to lead by a direct and easy way
2) to grant a successful issue, to cause to prosper
3) to prosper, be successful

All scriptures using *euodoo*:

> "Making request, if by any means now at length I might have a prosperous journey by the will of God to come unto you" (Rom. 1:10).

> "Upon the first day of the week let every one of you lay by him in store, as God hath prospered (2137) him, that there be no gatherings when I come" (1 Cor. 16:2).

> "Beloved, I wish above all things that thou mayest prosper and be in health, even as thy soul prospereth" (3 John 1:2).

About the Author

Martin Powell is presently a musician, minister, preacher, teacher, author and businessman. He was born in London, England. His grew up in Nottingham where he studied music—specializing in the clarinet, winning many prizes. Obtaining a music scholarship, he traveled to London to study with Georgina Dobree at the *Royal Academy of Music*, from 1981-1985, and with Guy Deplus, Professor at the *Paris Conservatoire*, from 1985-1986. In 1983, he went on to be the first clarinetist to win both the Hawke's clarinet prize and the John Solomon Wind Soloist prize in the same year. Also being awarded the Leslie Martin Scholarship for Clarinet; winner of the Nicholas Blake ensemble Prize; winner of a major award from the Ian Fleming Trust; and finalist in the Haverhill Sinfonia Soloist competition.

He first came to international recognition as a prize winner in the International Clarinet Congress Competition in London in 1984 and winning "Best Musician" in the International Christian Arts for God Competition 2007. He has gone on to perform in England, Germany, Austria, France, Italy, Spain and the USA. He was also the principal clarinet player with the Henry Wood Chamber Orchestra. His clarinet playing has brought him to the attention of many composers. He has given World Premieres of many pieces; both Peter Heron and Wilfred Josephs have written pieces for him. Wilfred Joseph's First and Second sonatas were written for Martin and dedicated to him. The two sonatas were given world premieres at St. John's Smith Square, and the Harrogate International Music festival. Peter's "Soundbites" being premiered at the Purcell Room on the South Bank in Septem-

ber 1996. Other first performances of works by Joseph Horo-
vitz, Mark Andrews, Barton Armstrong, David Llewelyn Green,
Christopher Steel and Marjoijn Anstey. Martin has performed
many concertos internationally and at home in the United Kingdom. He has also recorded the music of Debussy, Poulenc,
Stravinsky, and many other composers. As a committed Christian, Martin has dedicated all of his music to God including the
many songs the Lord has given to him.

Martin Powell came back to the Lord at the age of twenty-one
during the blossoming height of his music career. Being pas-
sionate to know God, and being obedient to the calling of the
Lord, he sacrificially laid down his clarinet playing in order to
know the Lord and to spend time deeply studying the Scriptures,
which he has studied intensively for many years.

The Lord then took Martin into business, inspiring him to believe in a three story music store, which the Lord gave him when
he was penniless. Now Martin is promoting other Christians in
business with the website ChurchTalents.com.

From 1993 to 2010 Martin was the Pastor of the New Haven
Fellowship in London. This led to many preaching engagements
across the wide spectrum of denominations and independent
churches. His preaching has also been transmitted on the Gospel
Channel through the Sky Satellite Network.

Out of his study of the Scriptures, the Lord began to give him
fresh revelation about the subject of money. In obedience to the
Lord, Martin Powell has written this book about money matters
in God's Kingdom that is now in your hands. It is full of the living Word of God which he prays will be a blessing to you as you
apply the principles of this book to your life.

Supplemental Material Available Soon

Please write to us at: info@Kingdom-Talents.com if you are interested in purchasing the *Money Matters: In My Kingdom Study Guide,* or "Money Matters: In My Kingdom".

To correspond with Martin Powell, please send your letter via email to: info@Kingdom-Talents.com. You may also contact us in writing at: Martin Powell, c/o Kingdom Talents, 375 Star Light Drive, Fort Mill, SC 29715.

We would love to hear from you, and welcome your comments. If you desire Martin to come and minister the Word of God and perform his music in your Church, please mention this when you write.

Made in the USA
Middletown, DE
30 June 2019